Colorblind Free

JH Fleming

Joseph Fleming

Original Photography

Decades of being around accomplished talent producing absolutely phenomenal quality work has taught that we are capable of greatness. It is possible to meet our destiny and become it. Experiencing excellence done with such apparent ease and humble selfless gratification is the motivation for this photography. Most important was having the freedom.

Being colorblind gives an advantage when composing black & white... less confusion. This special collection selected from thousands of captures. All images were framed in the camera and presented without edits, genuine as seen through the lens. Panchromatic conversion applied by unique proprietary process.

Limited prints and custom work available.

info@ BEACHNOISE.com

JH FLEMING

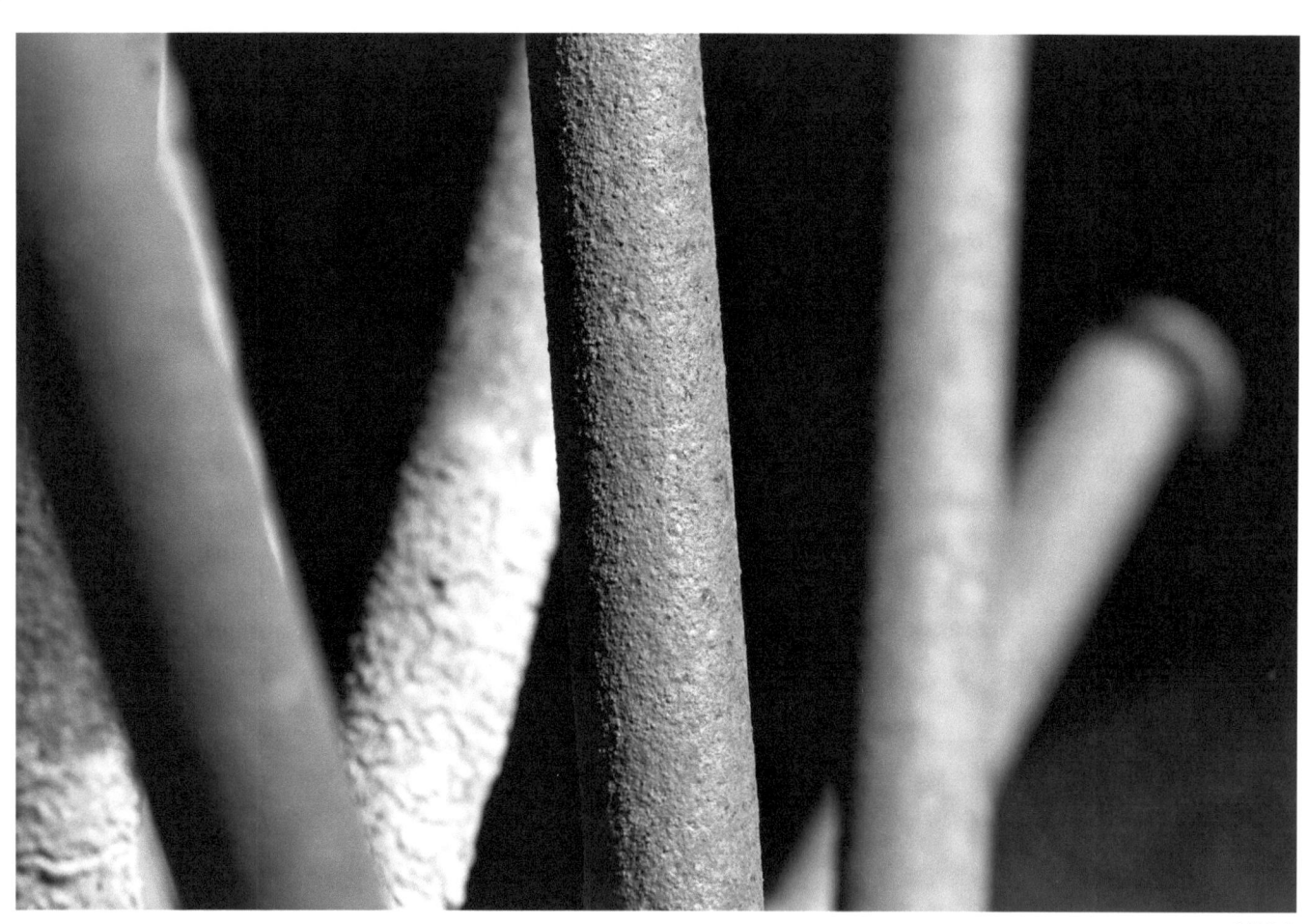

0780

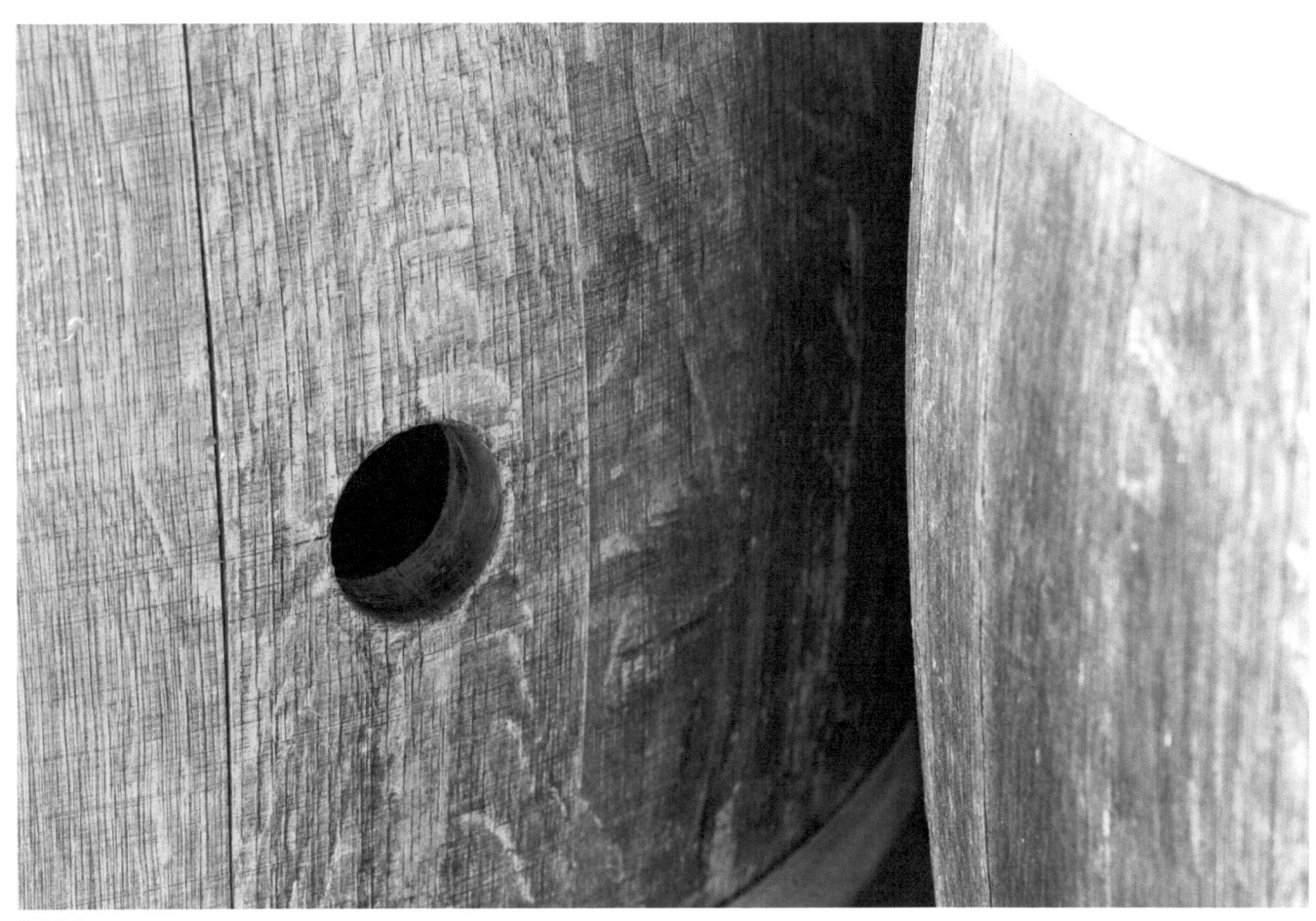

0826

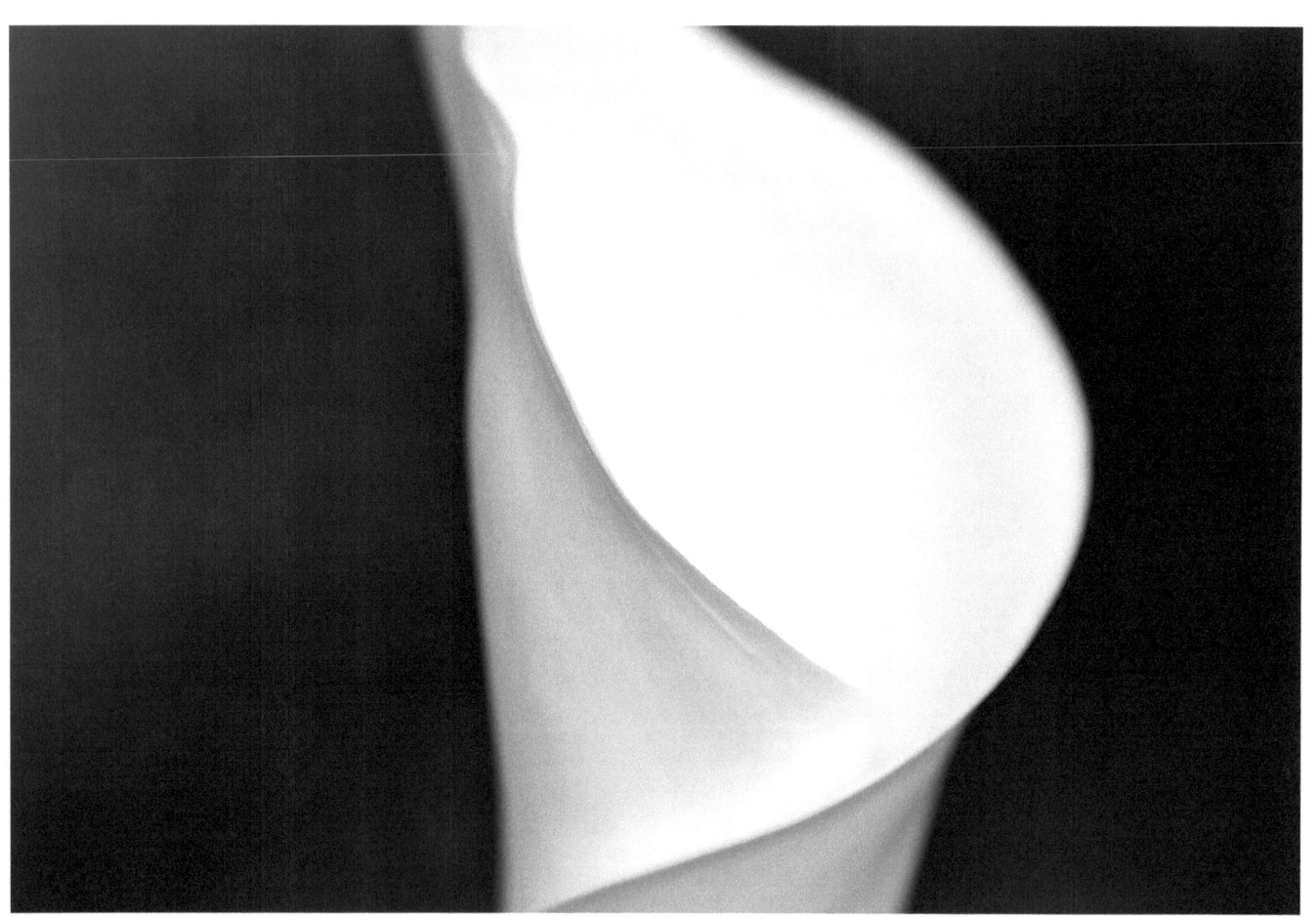

0920

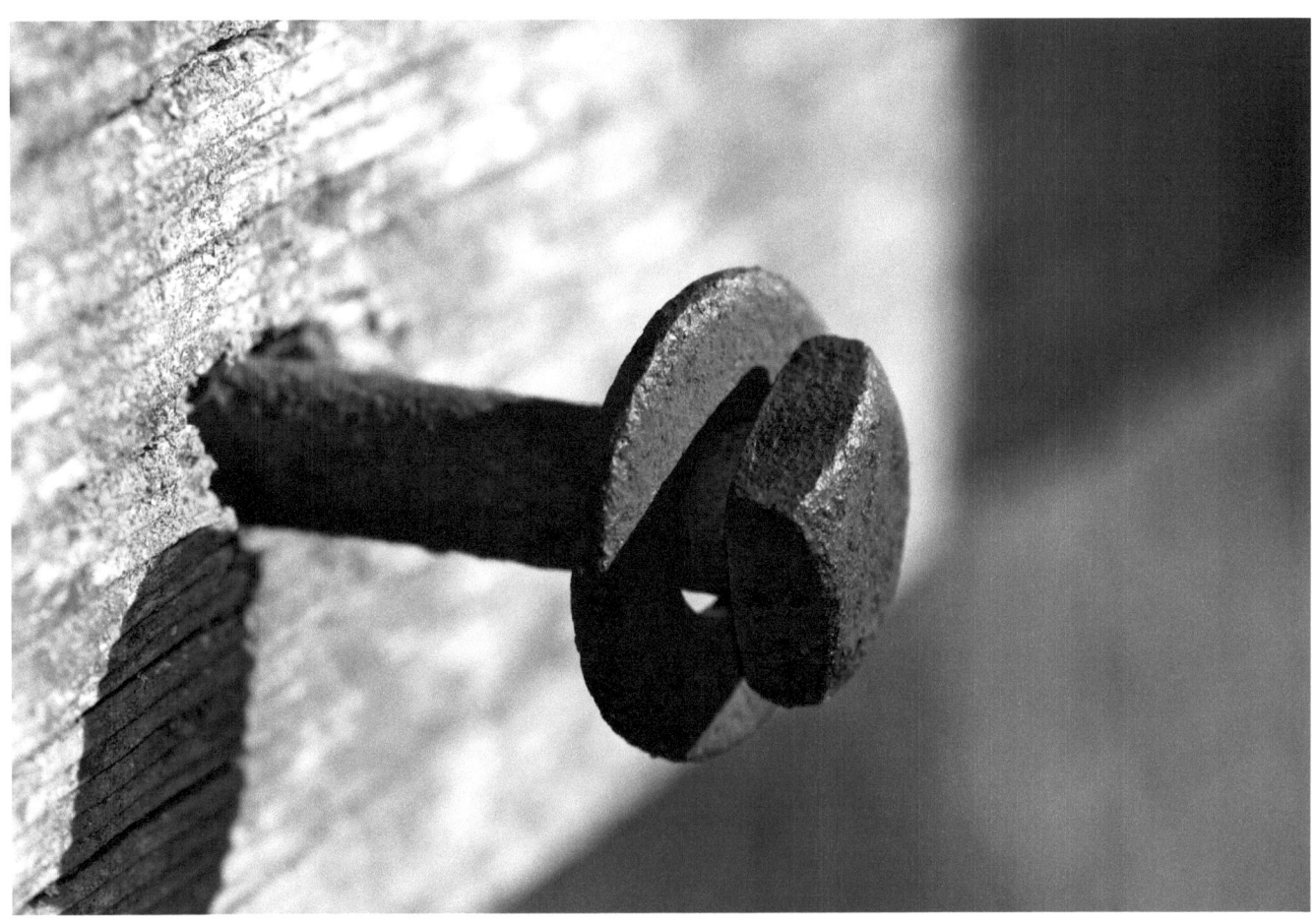

1173

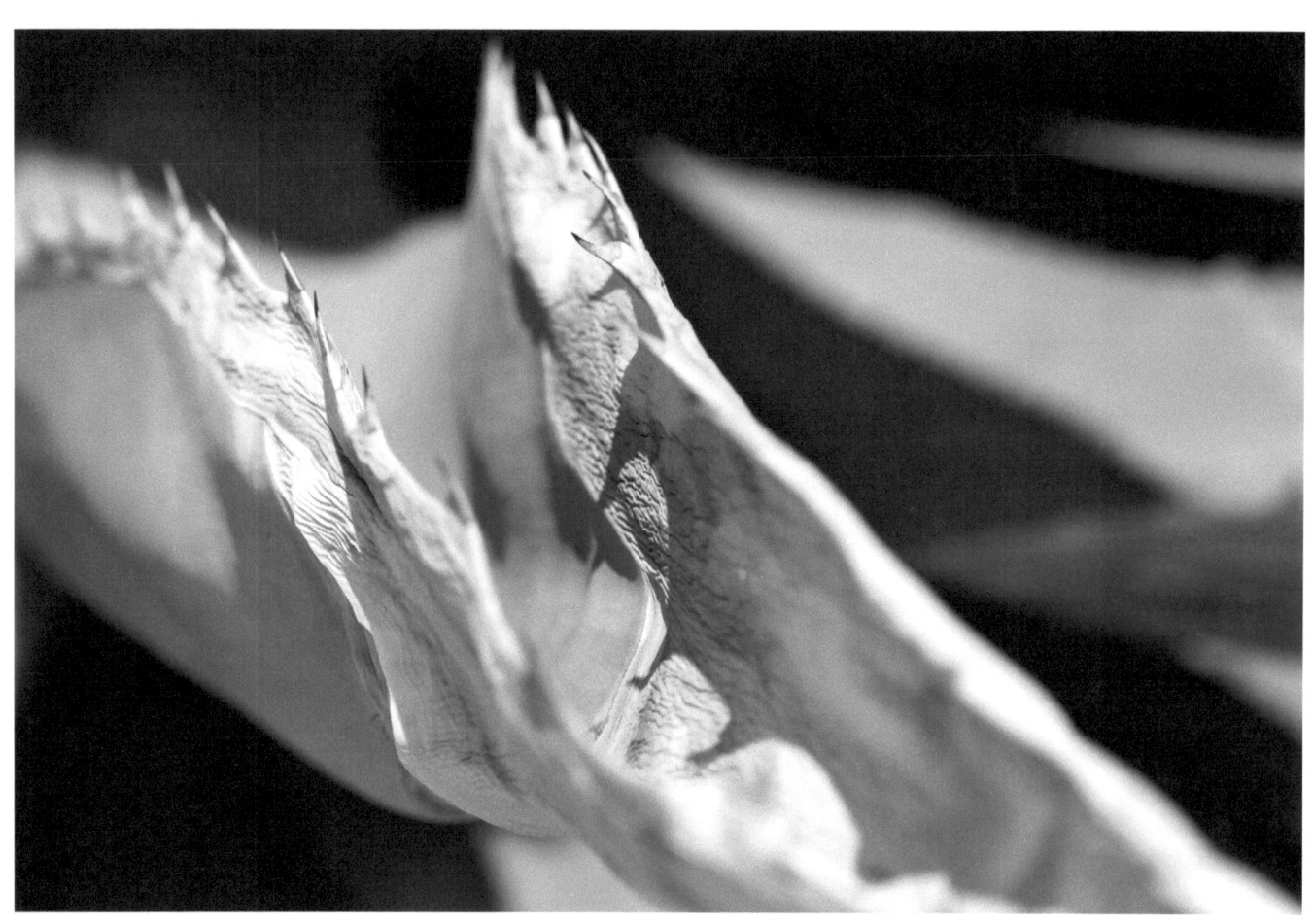

1581

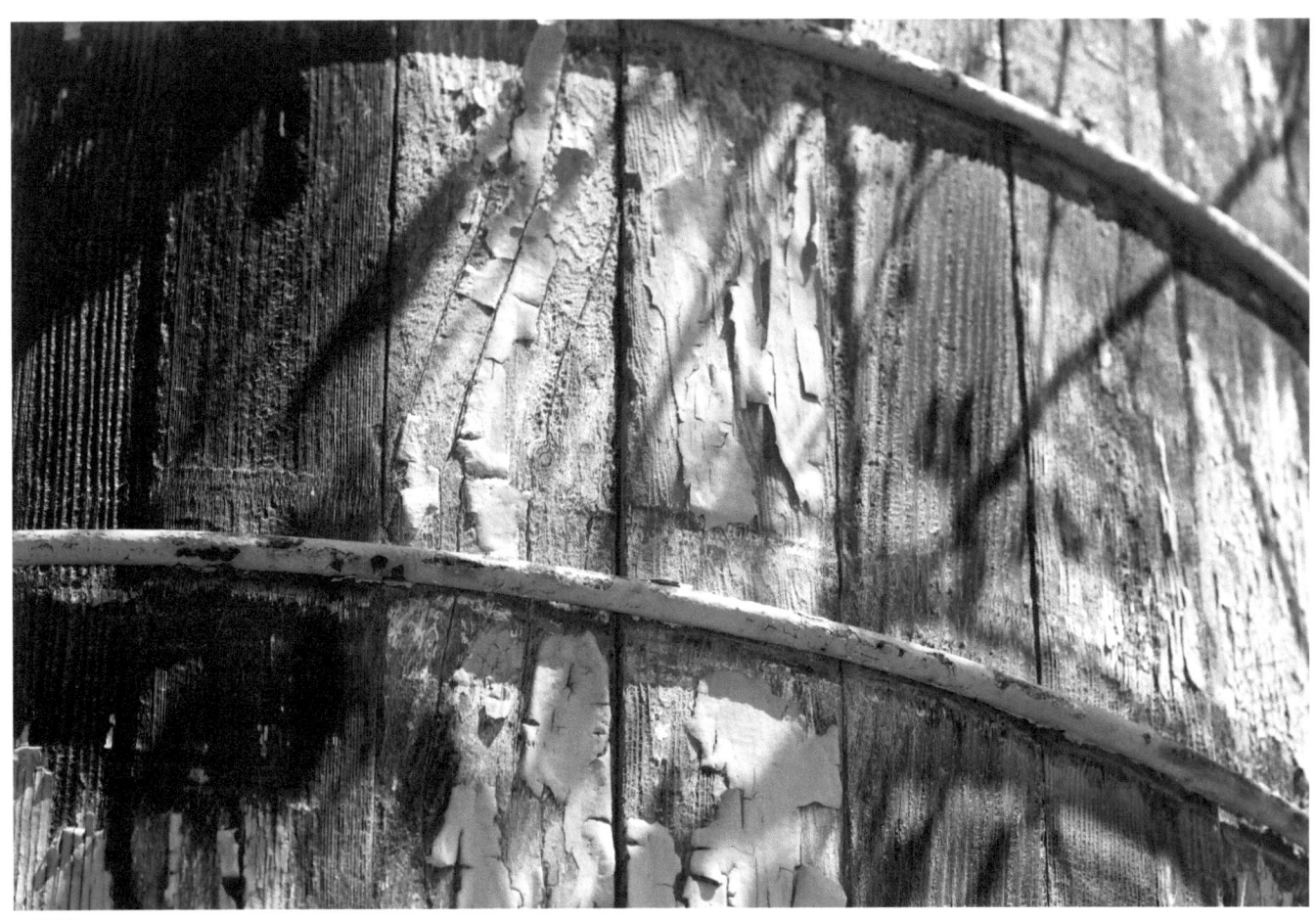

1608

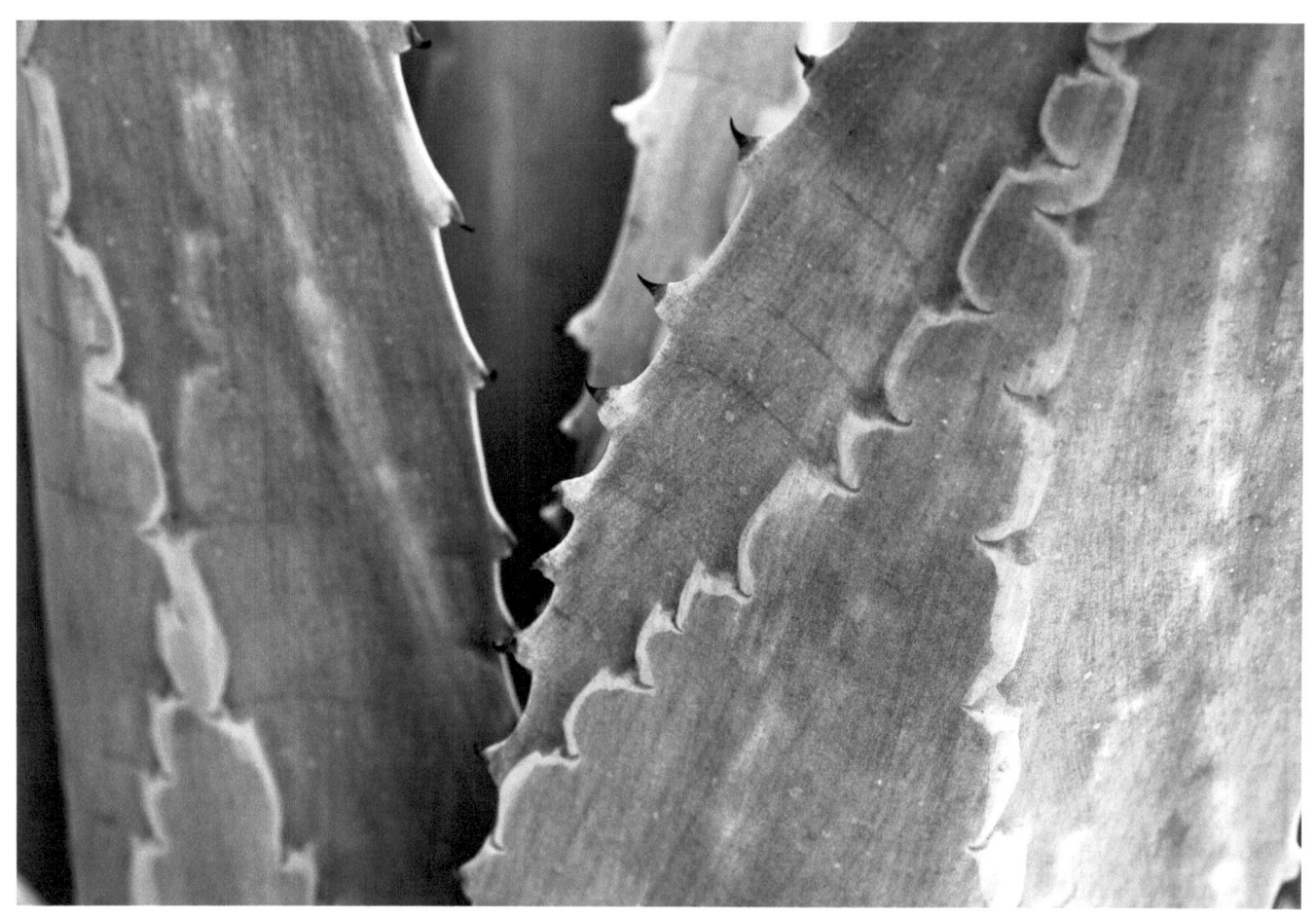

1976

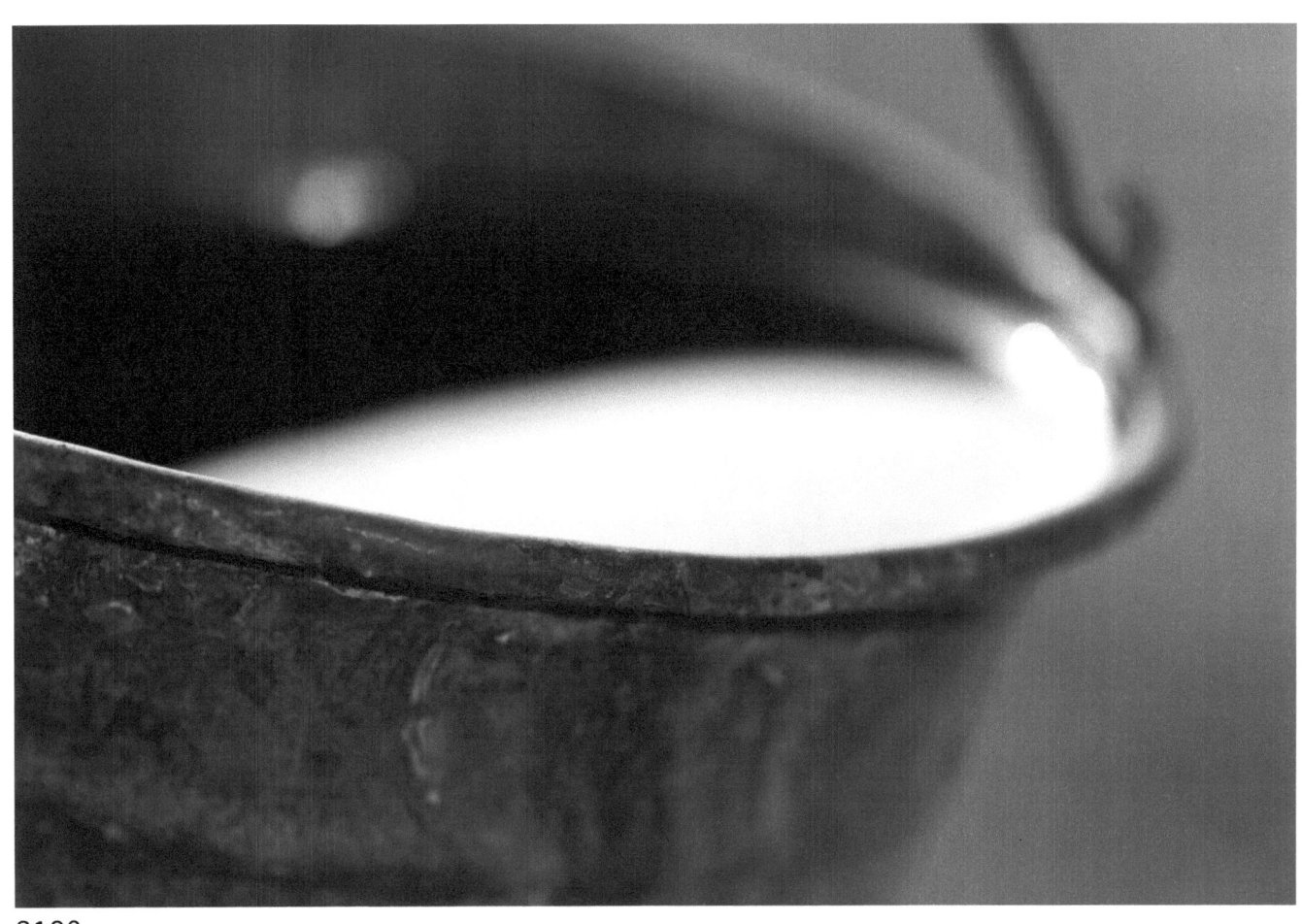

2180

2397

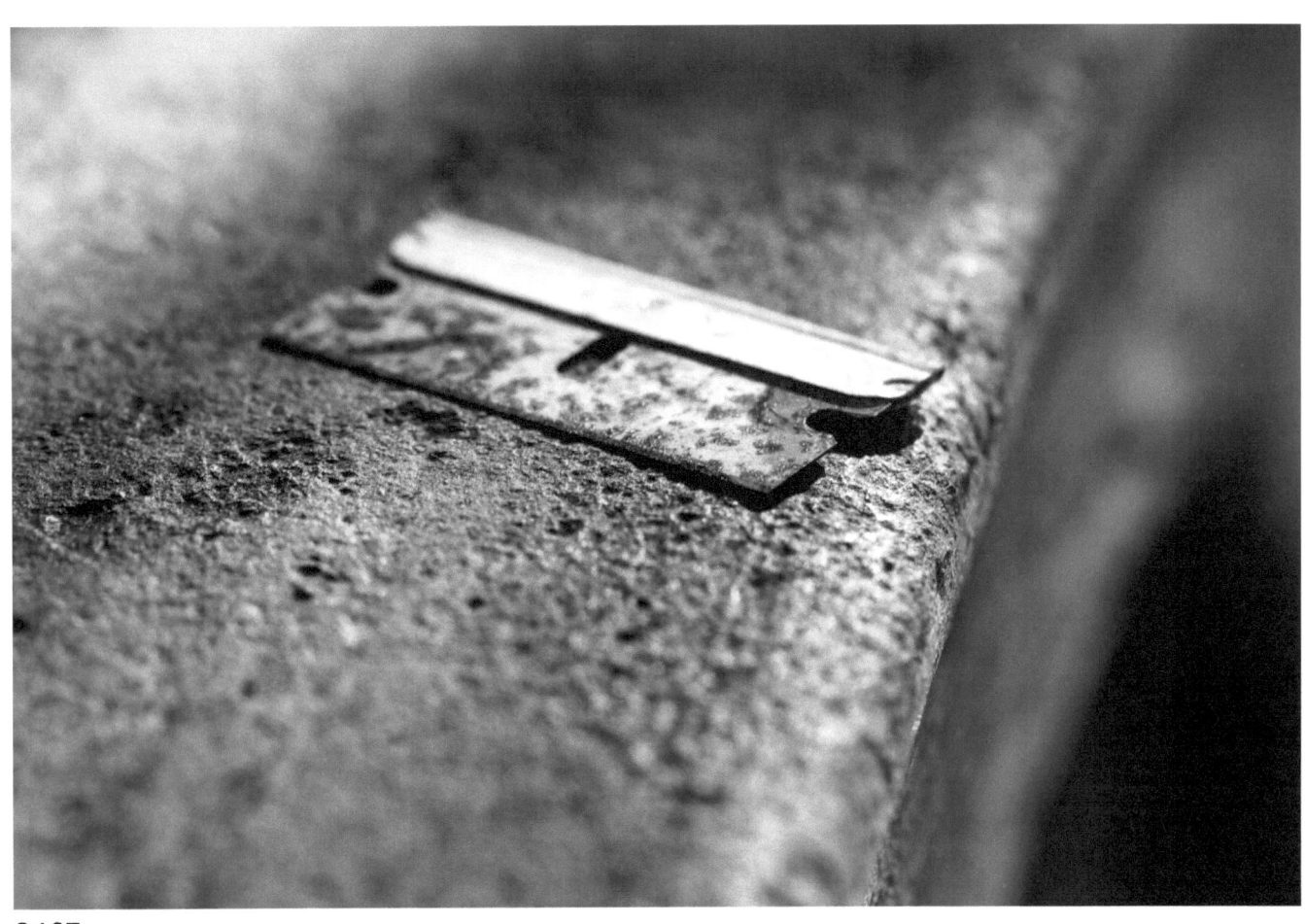

2467

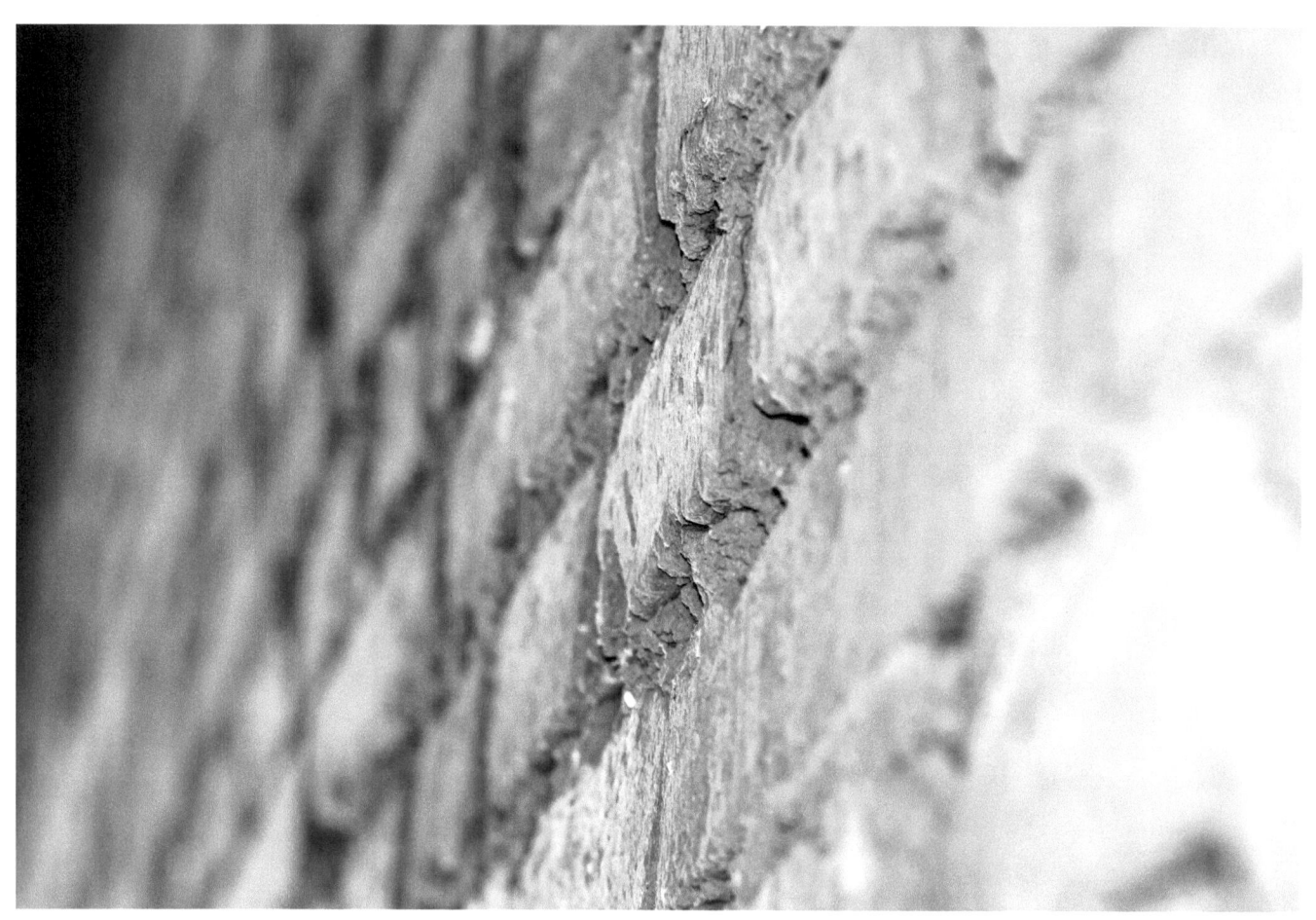

2688

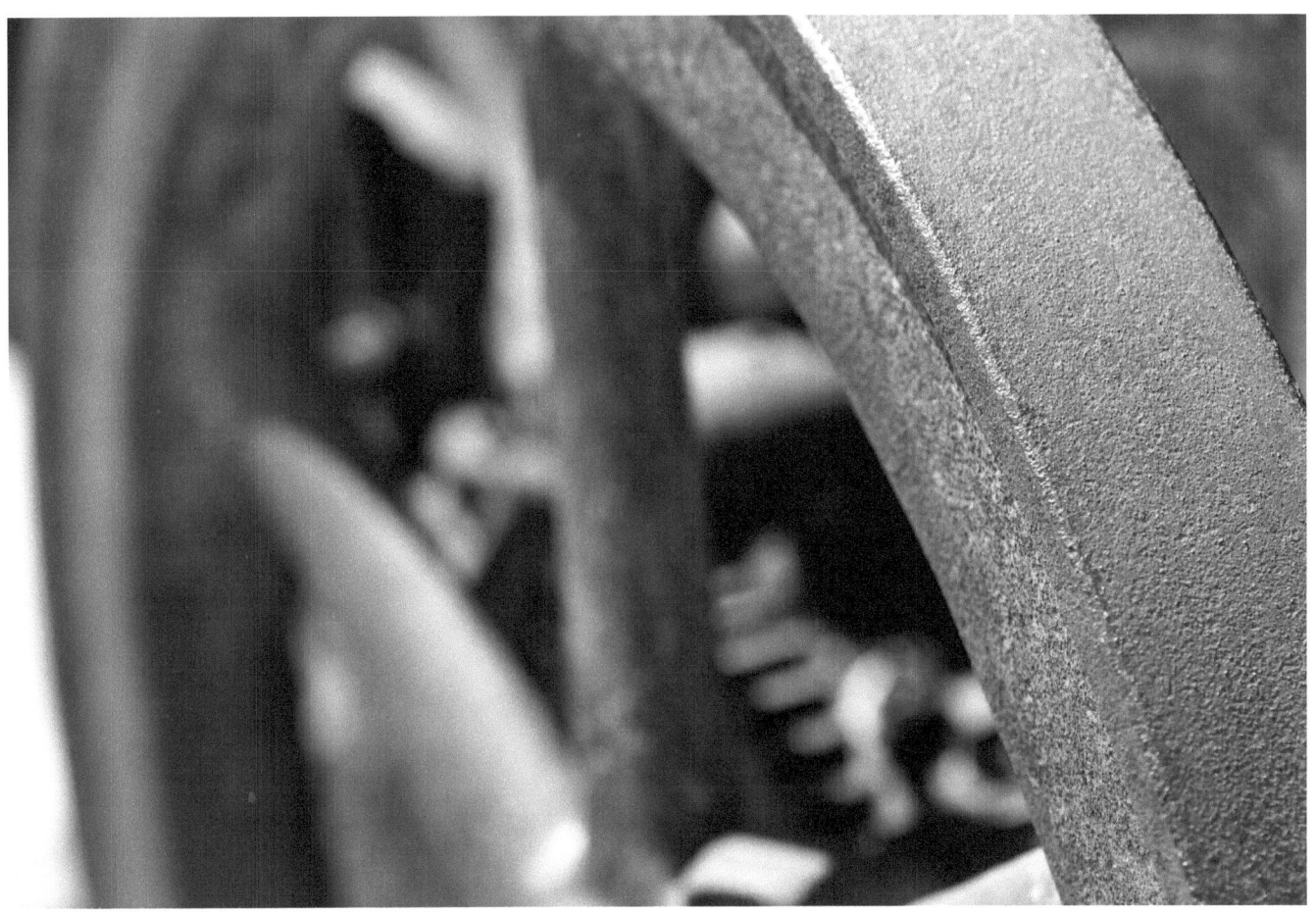

2962

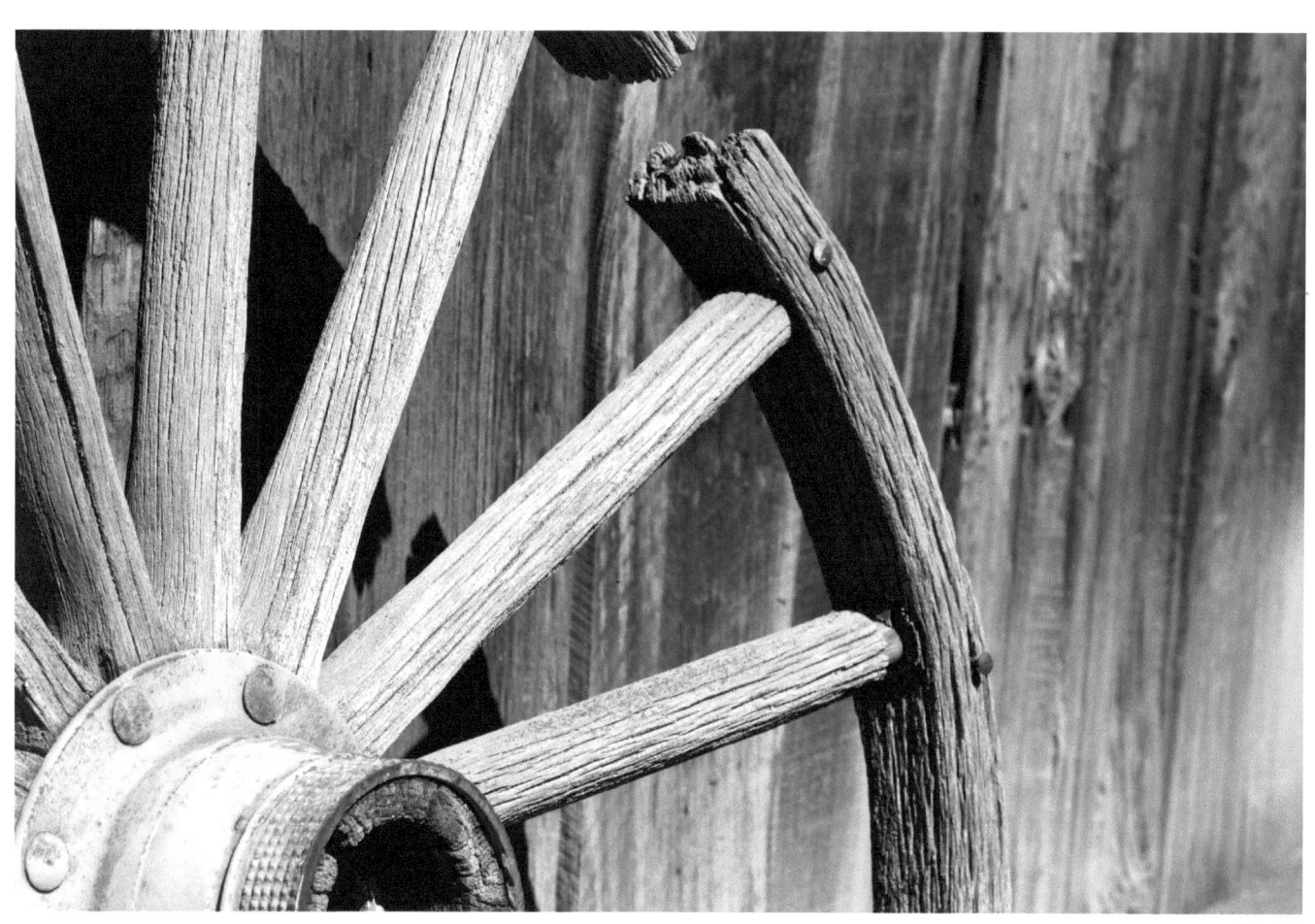

3147

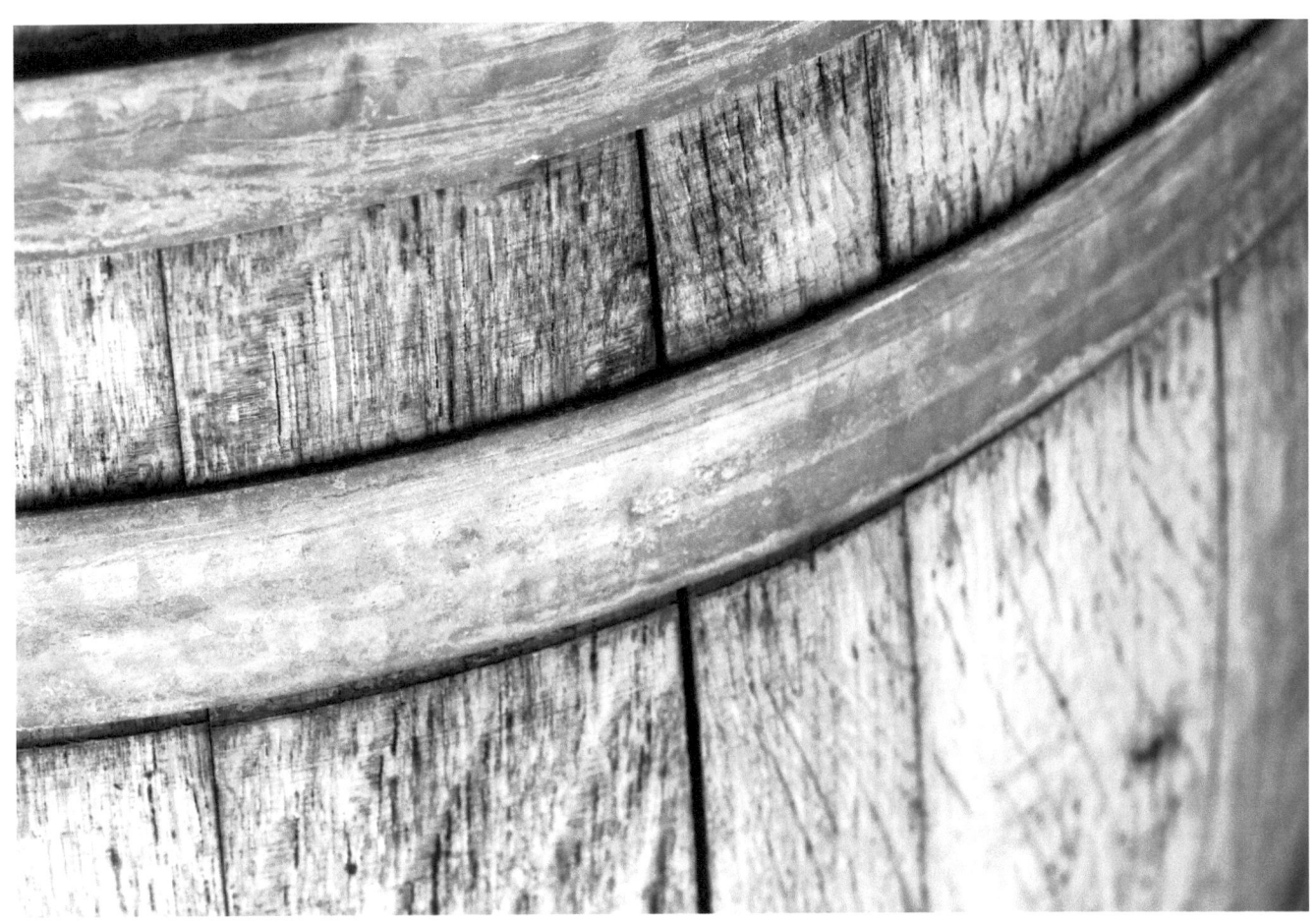

3151

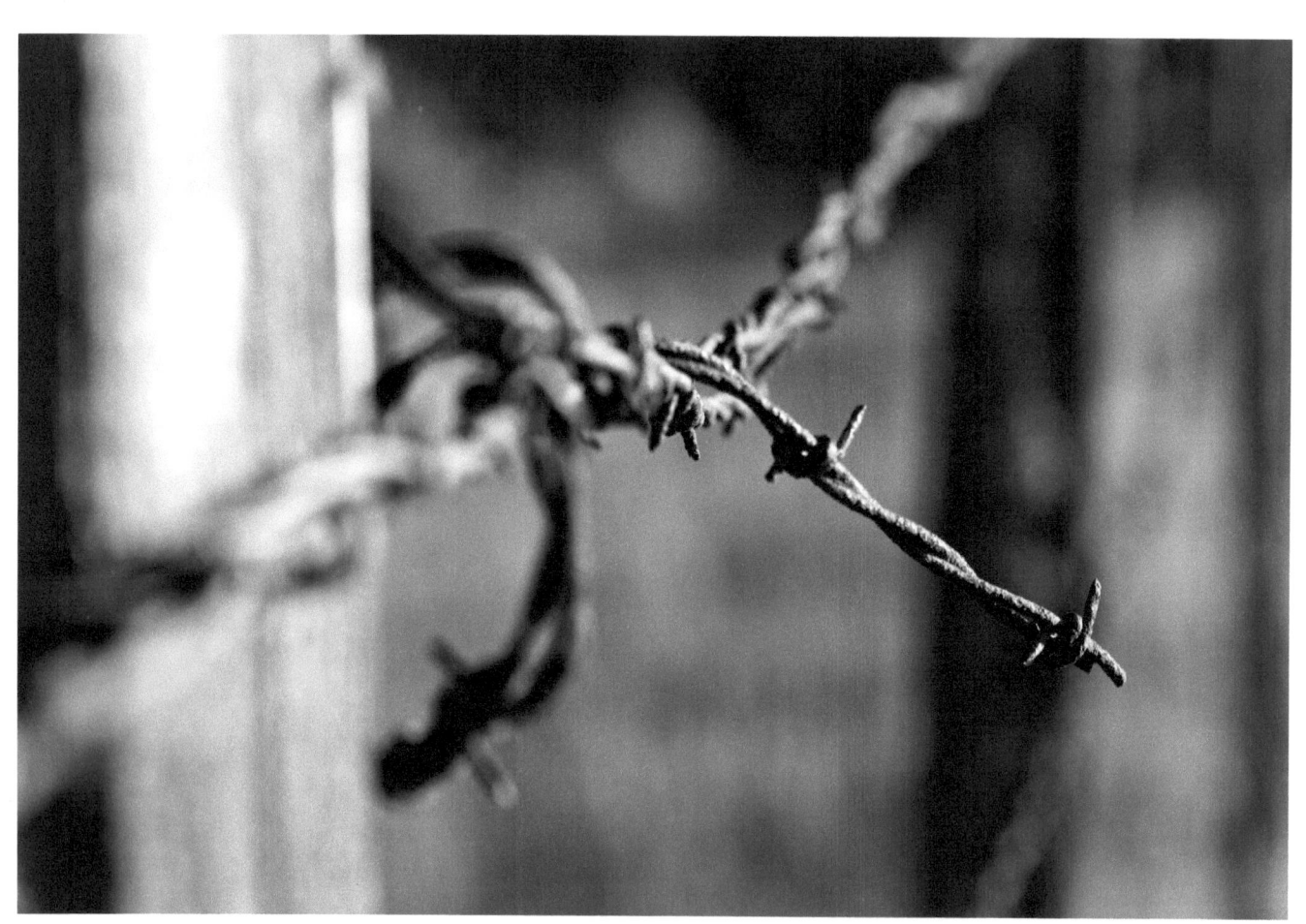

3359

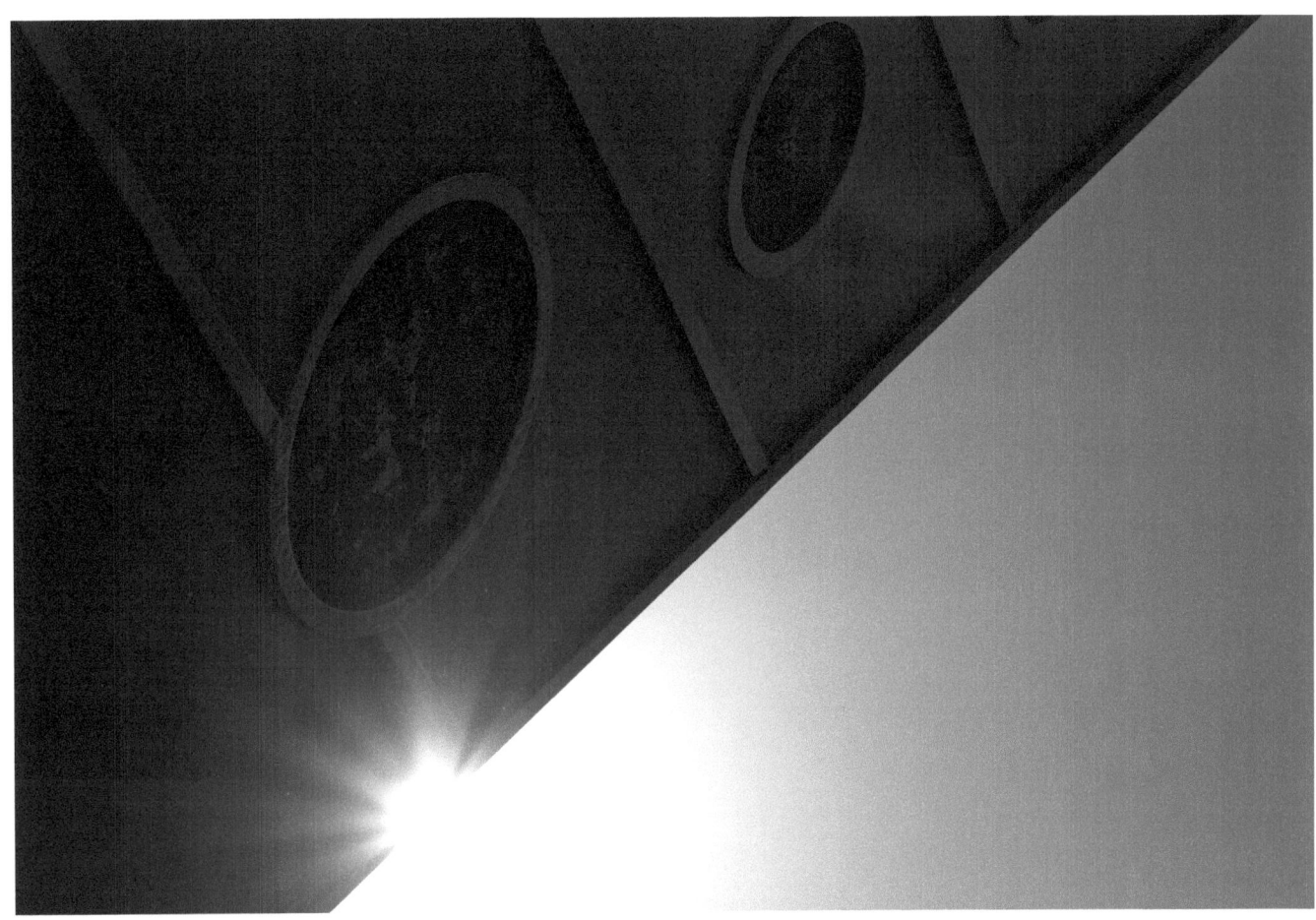

3621

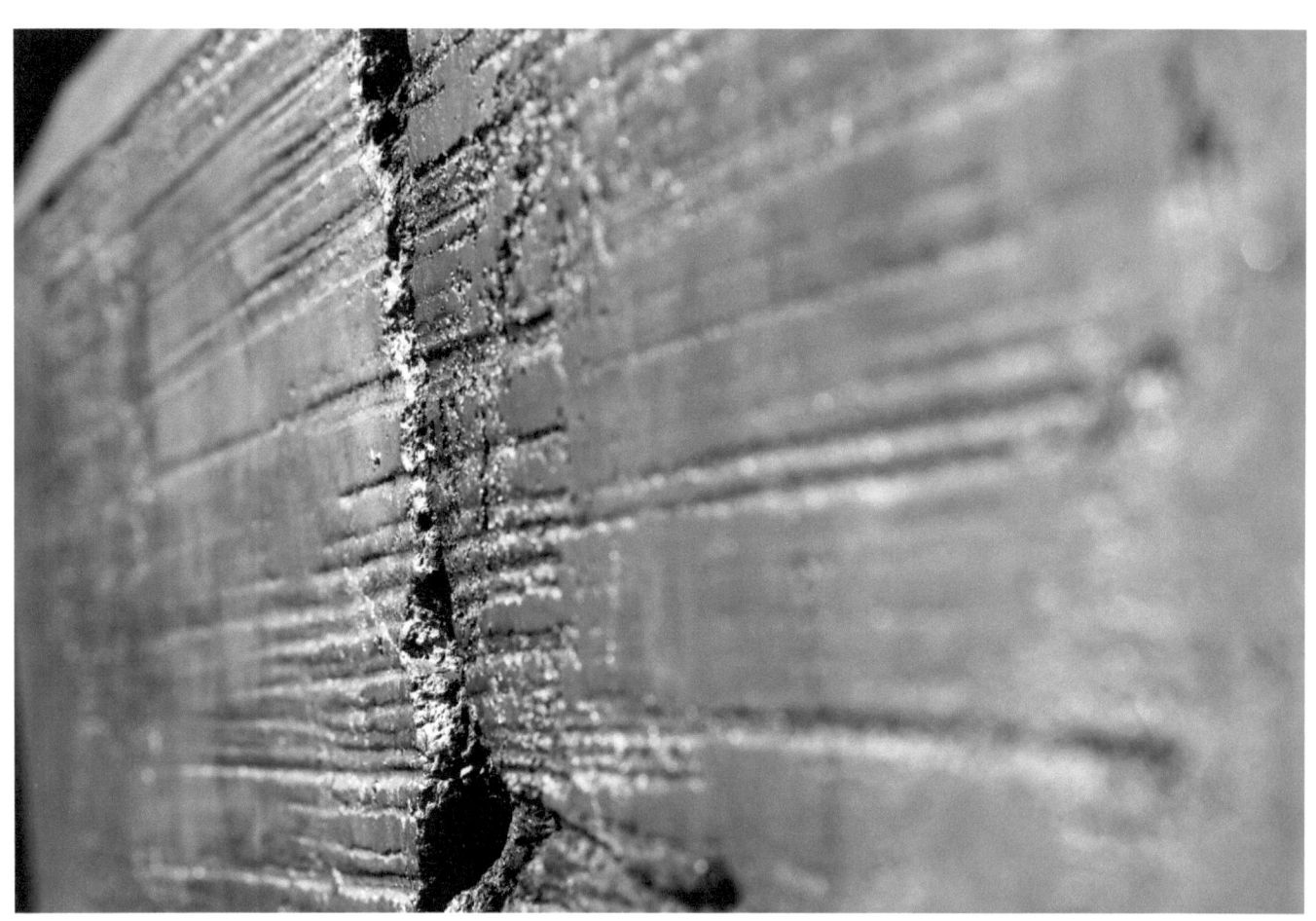

3656

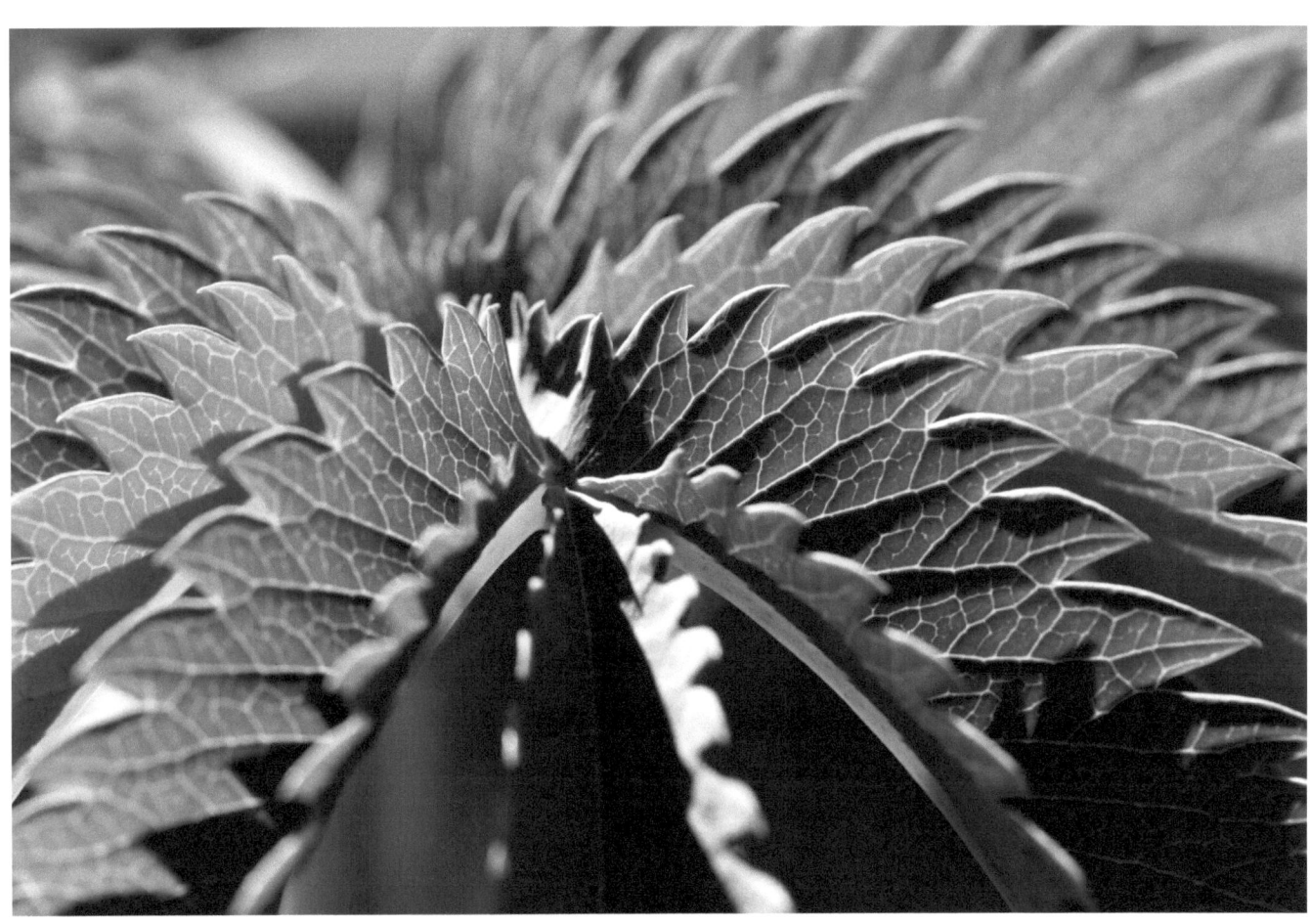

3714

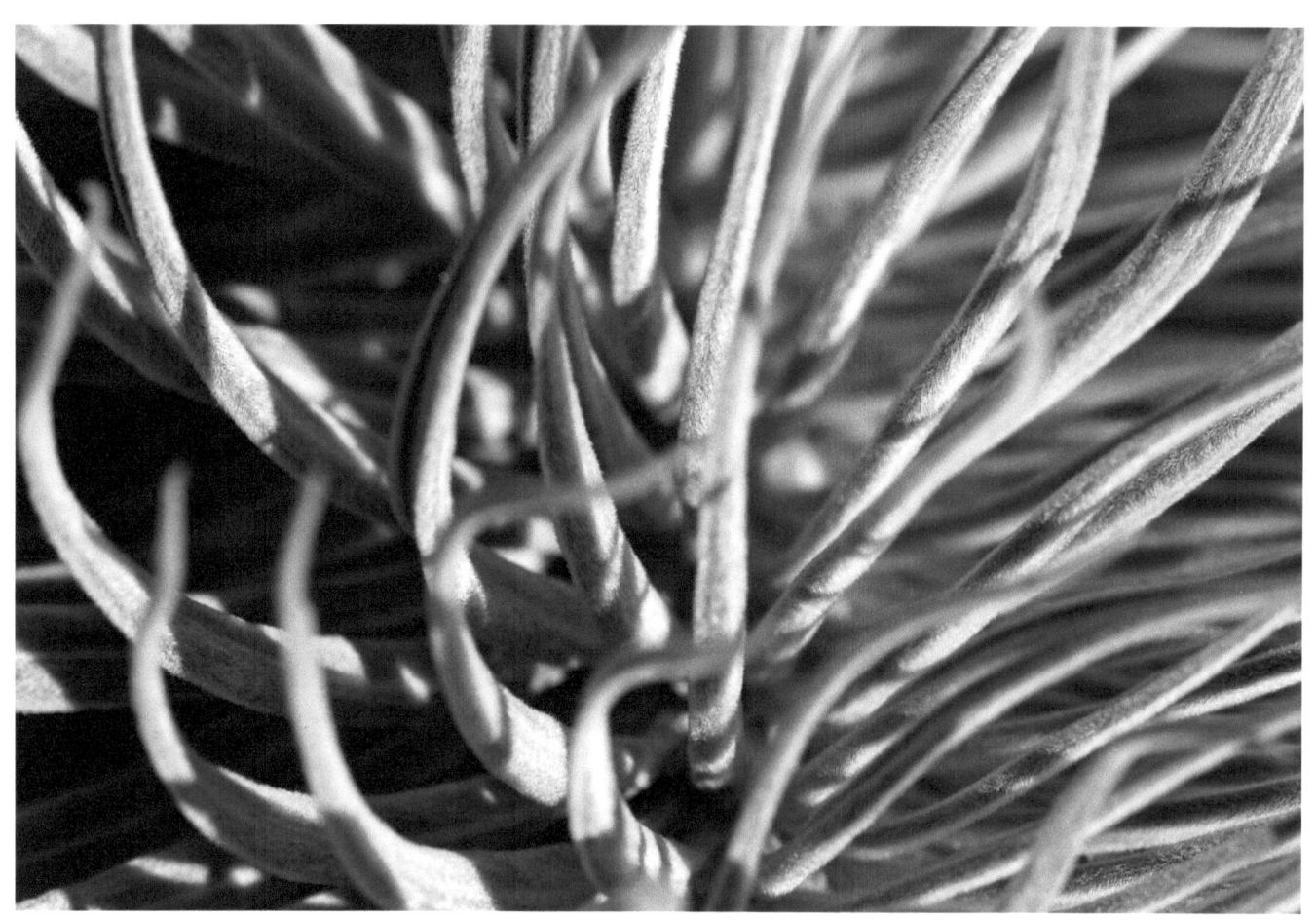

3752

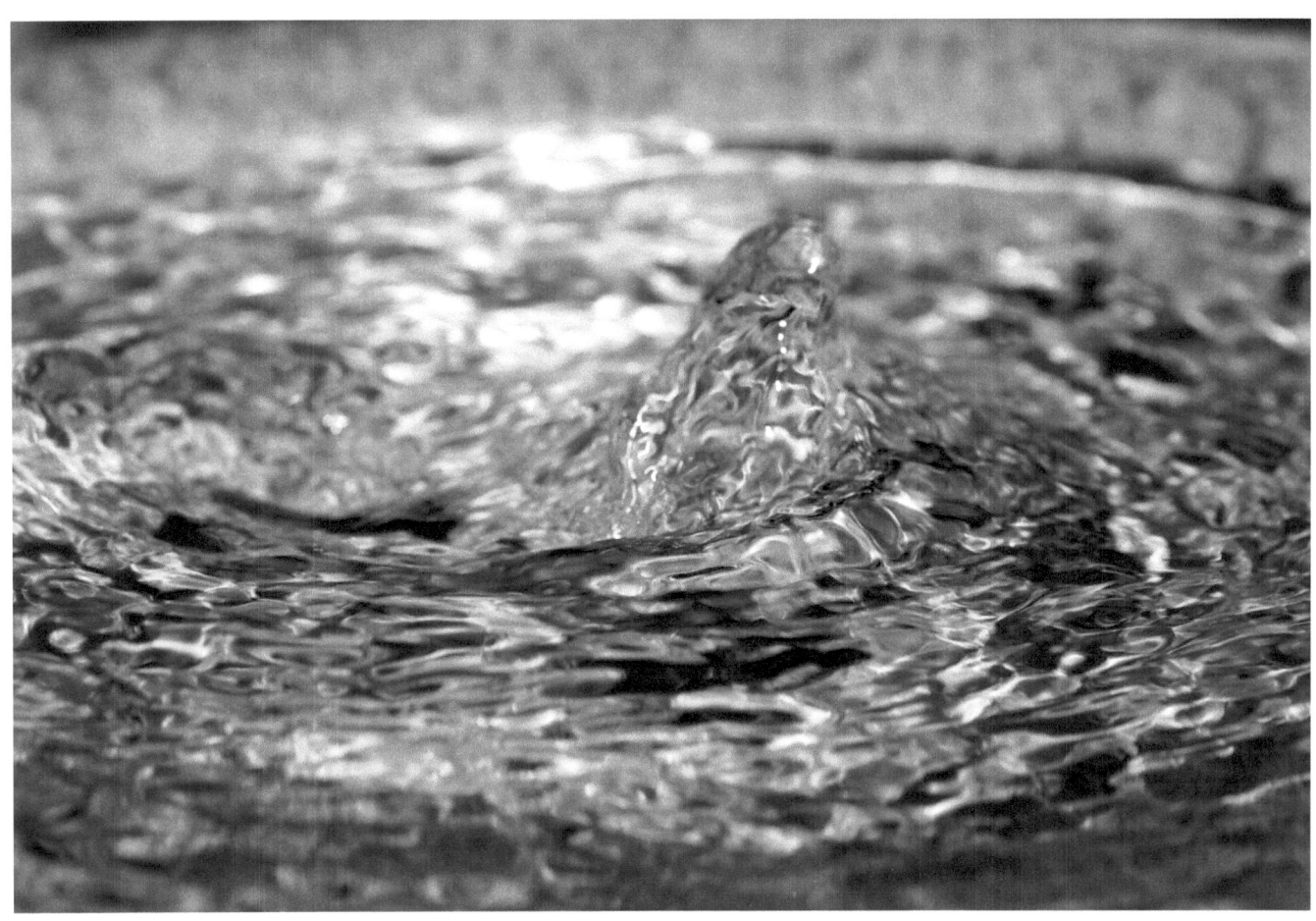

3795

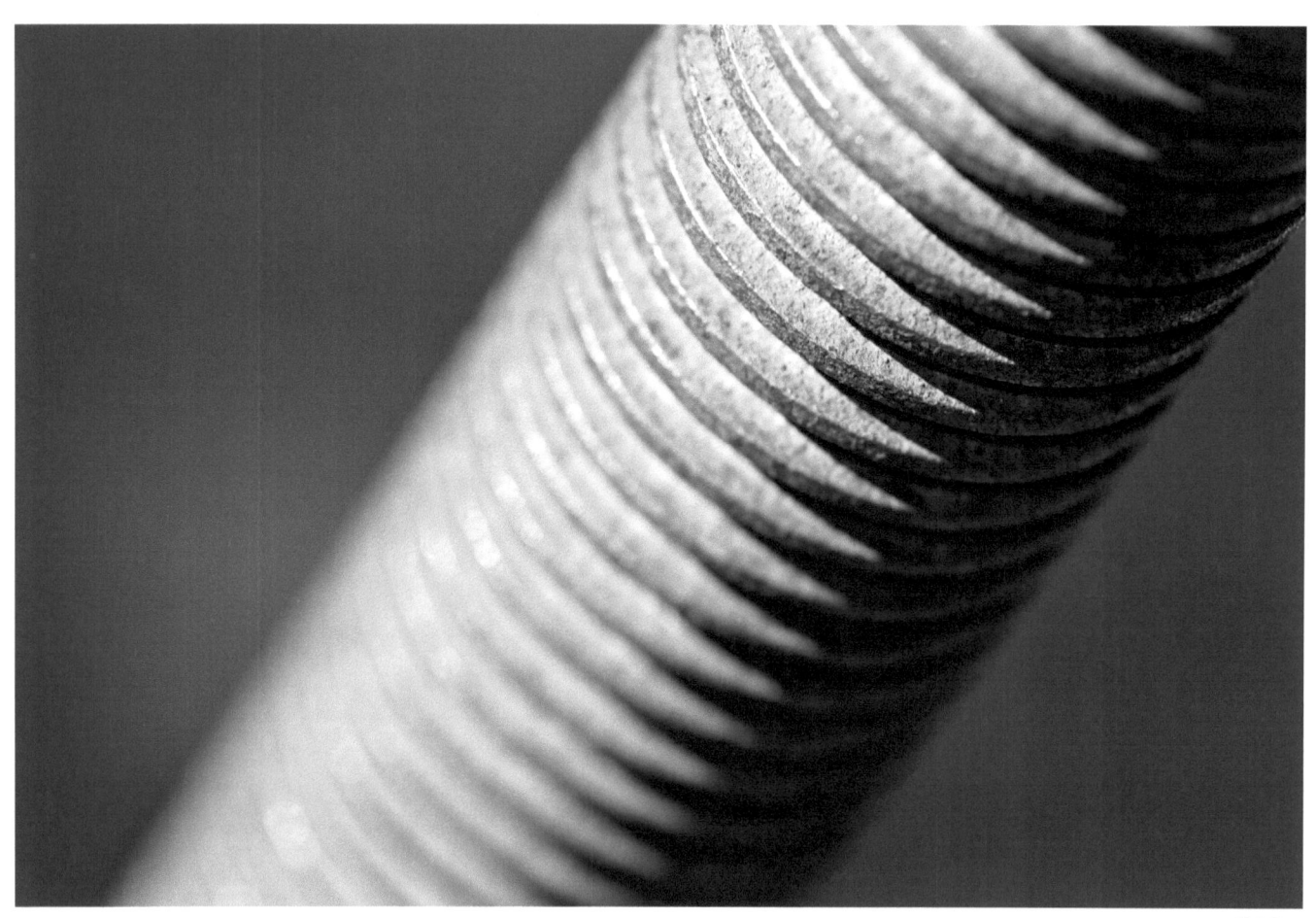

3937

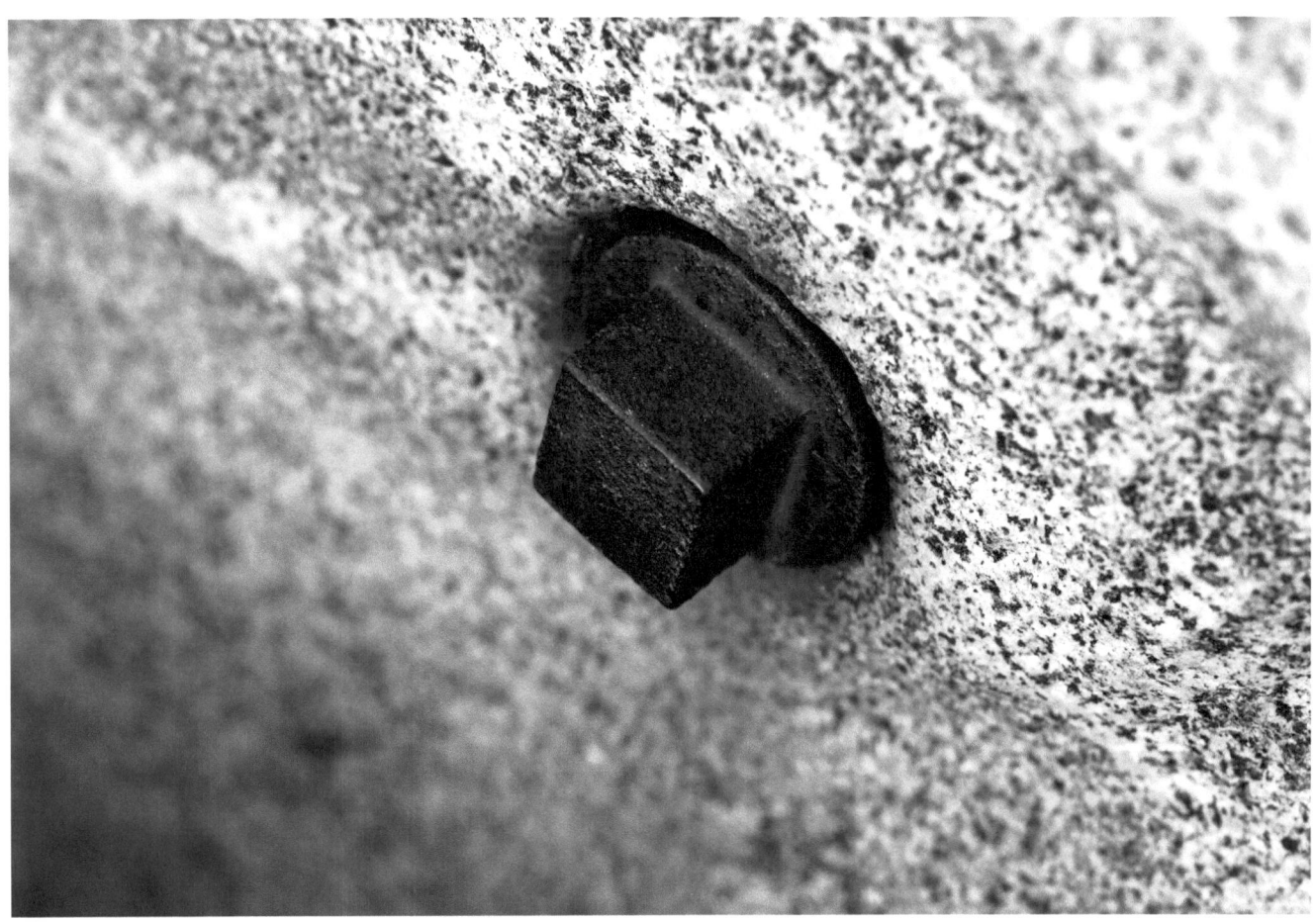

4035

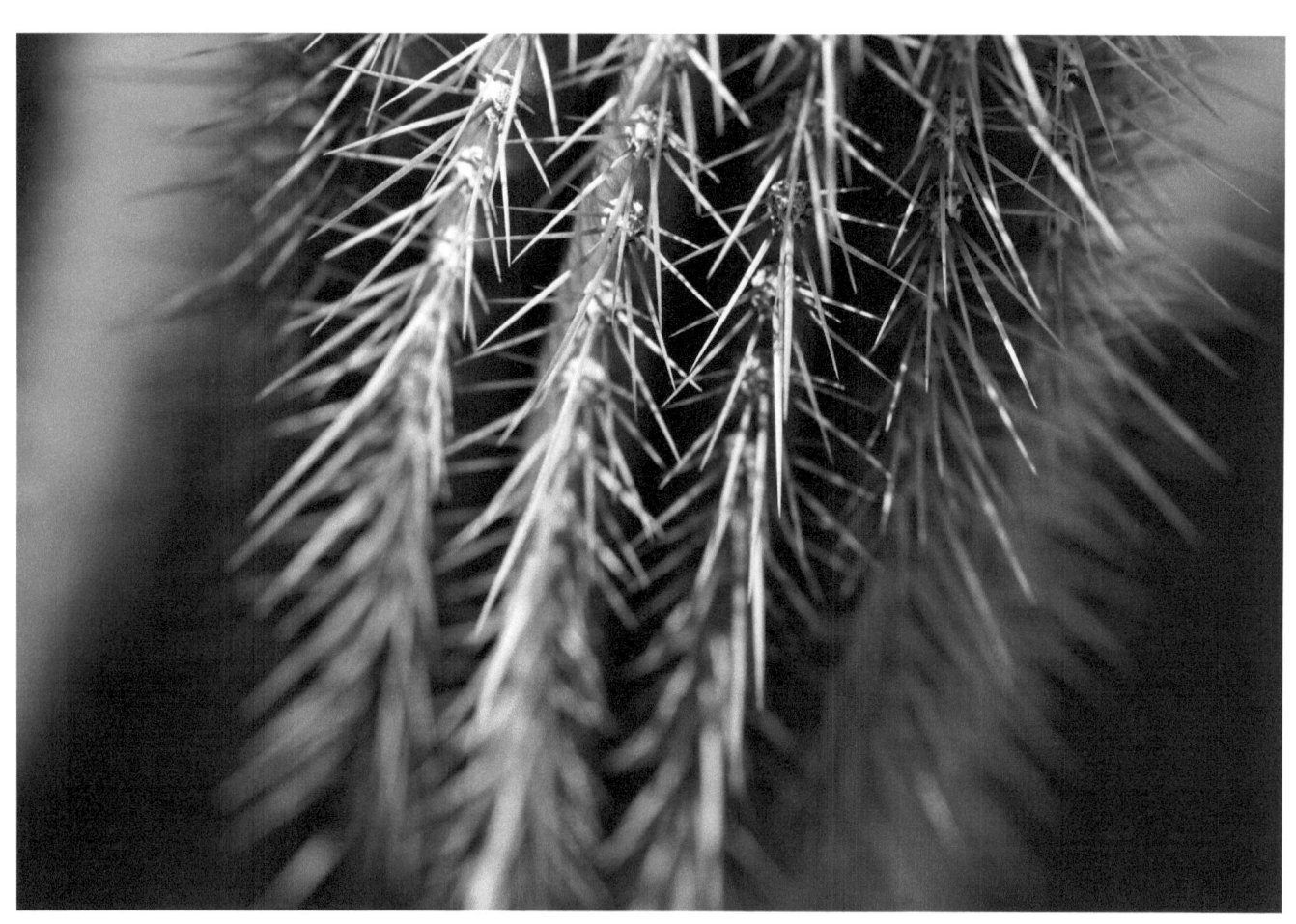

4070

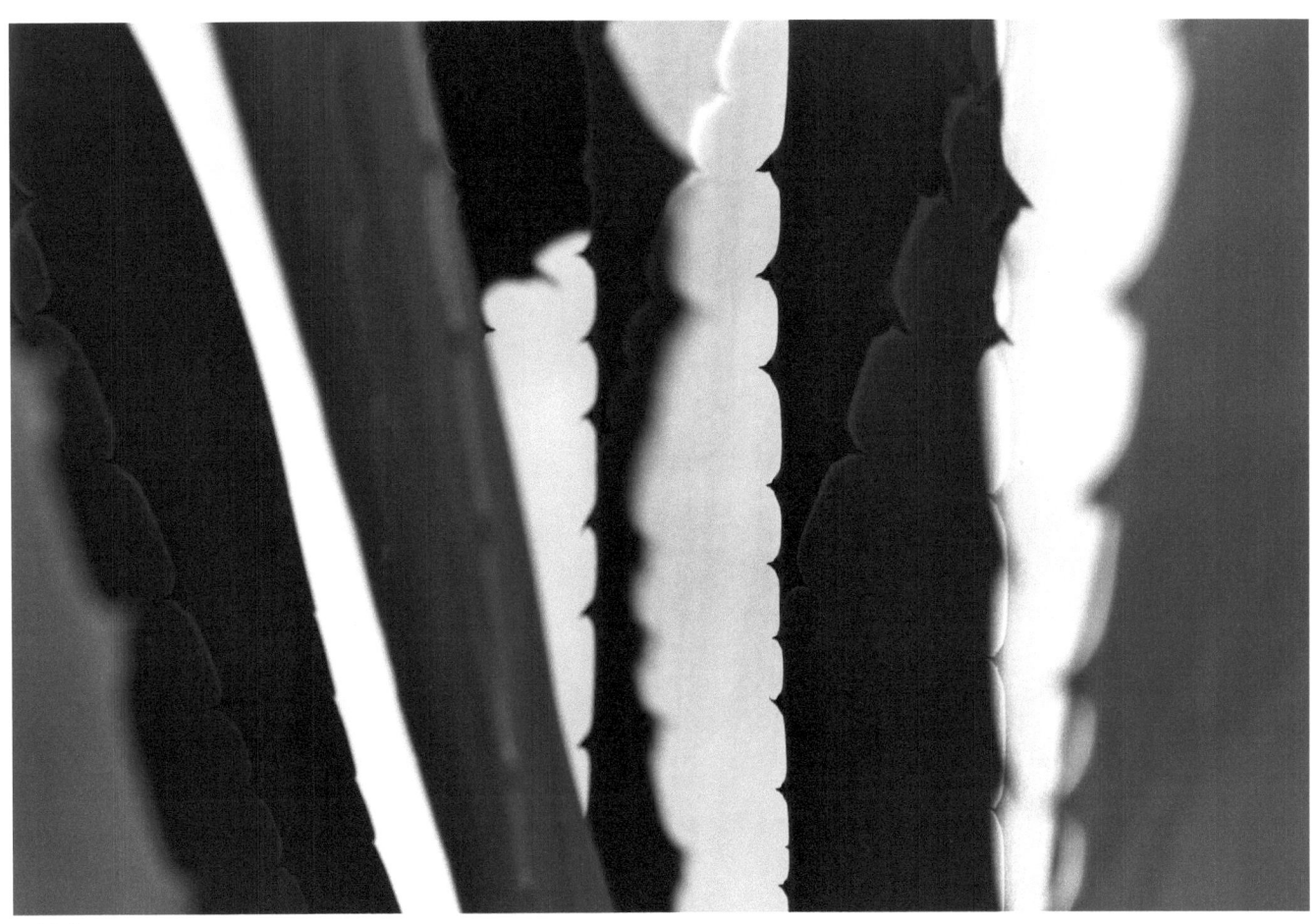

4099

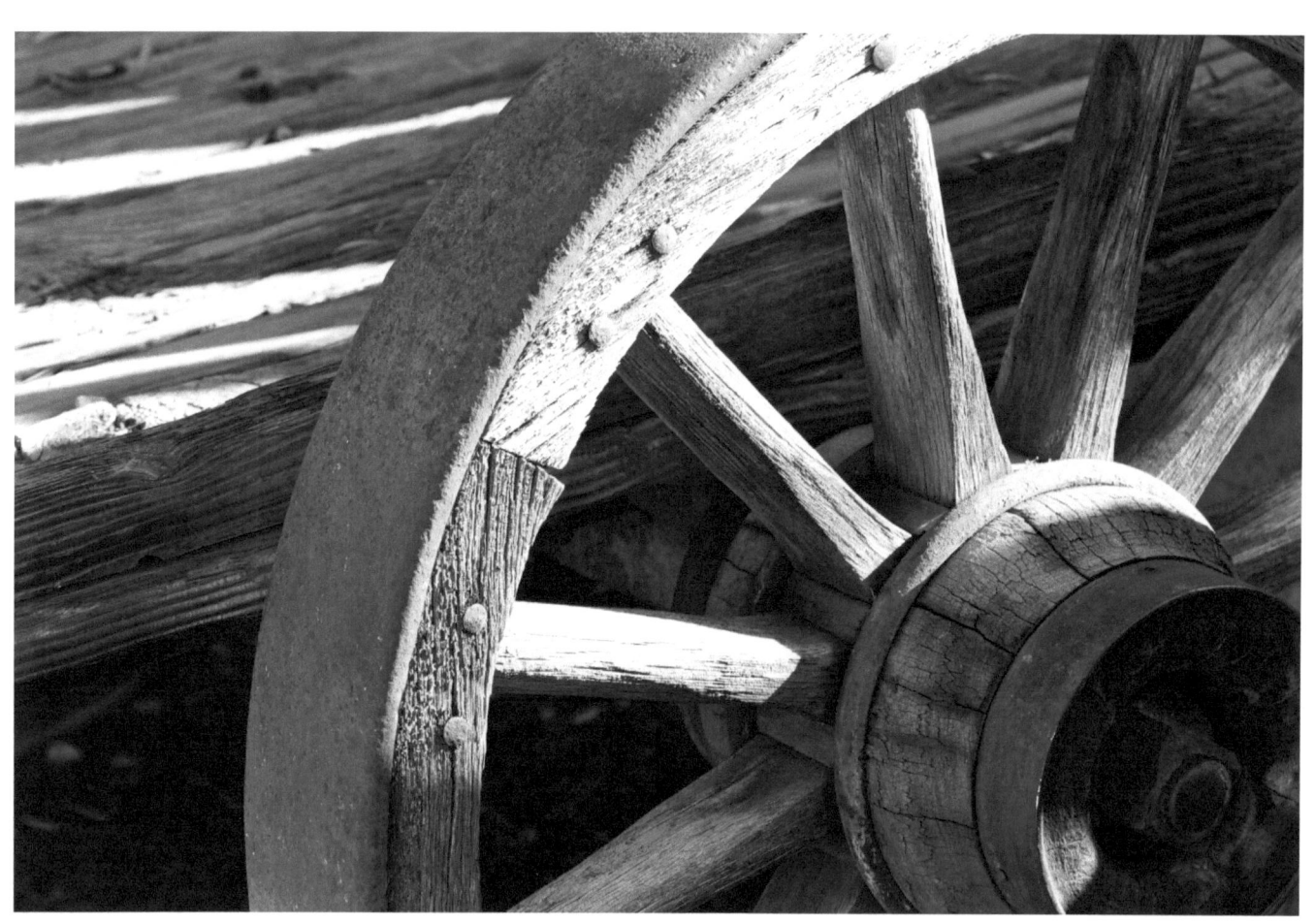

4128

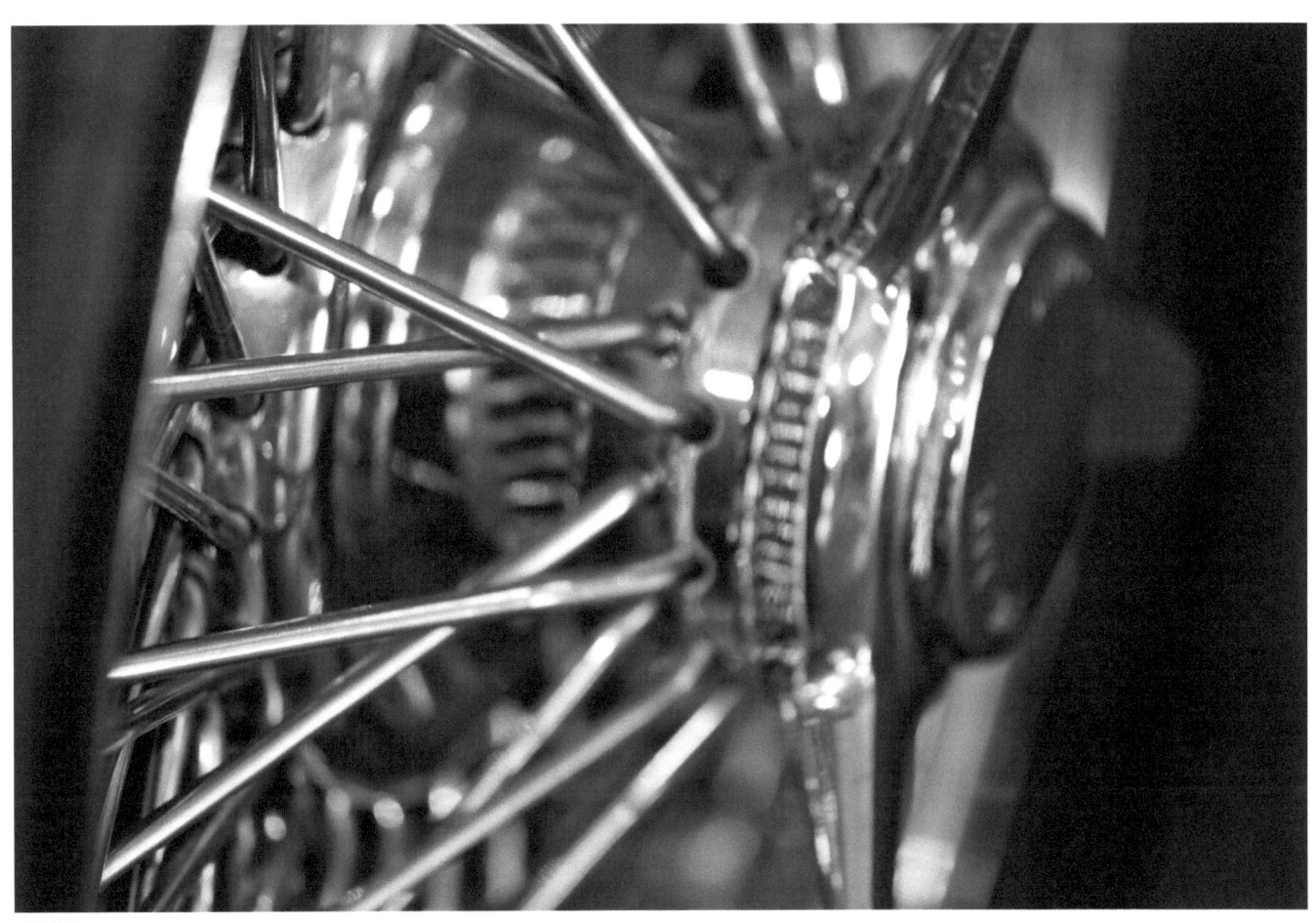

4193

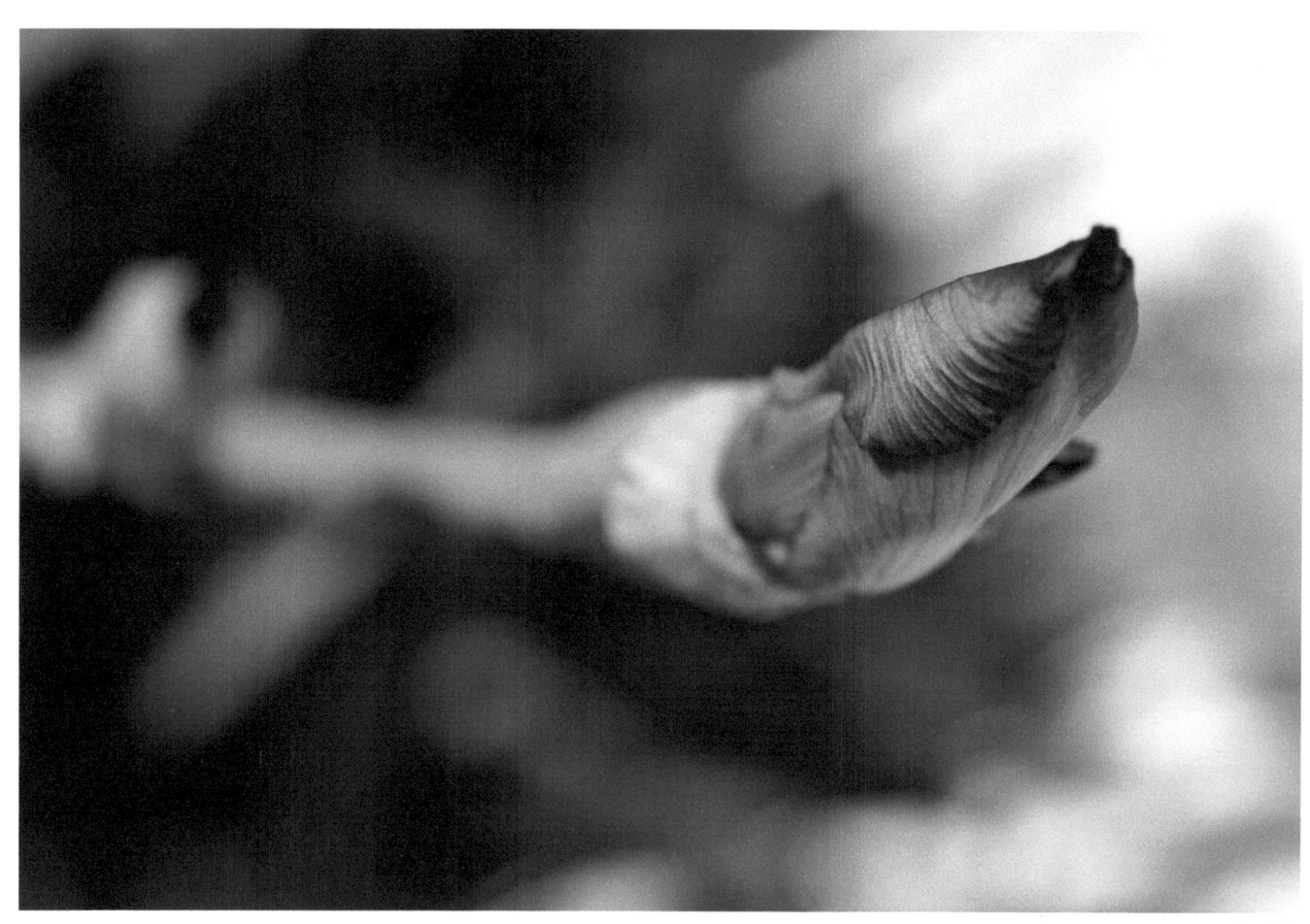

5492

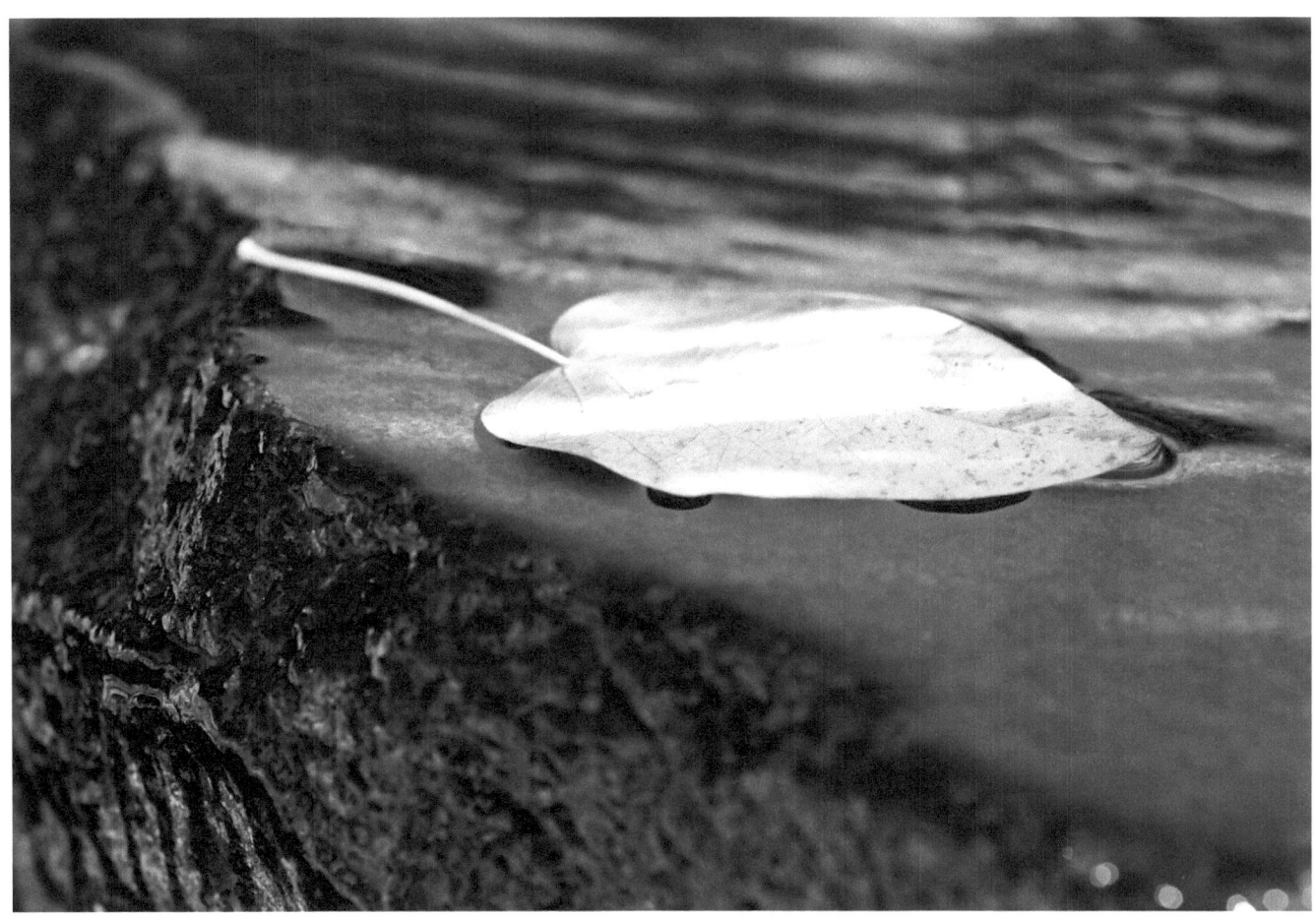

5750

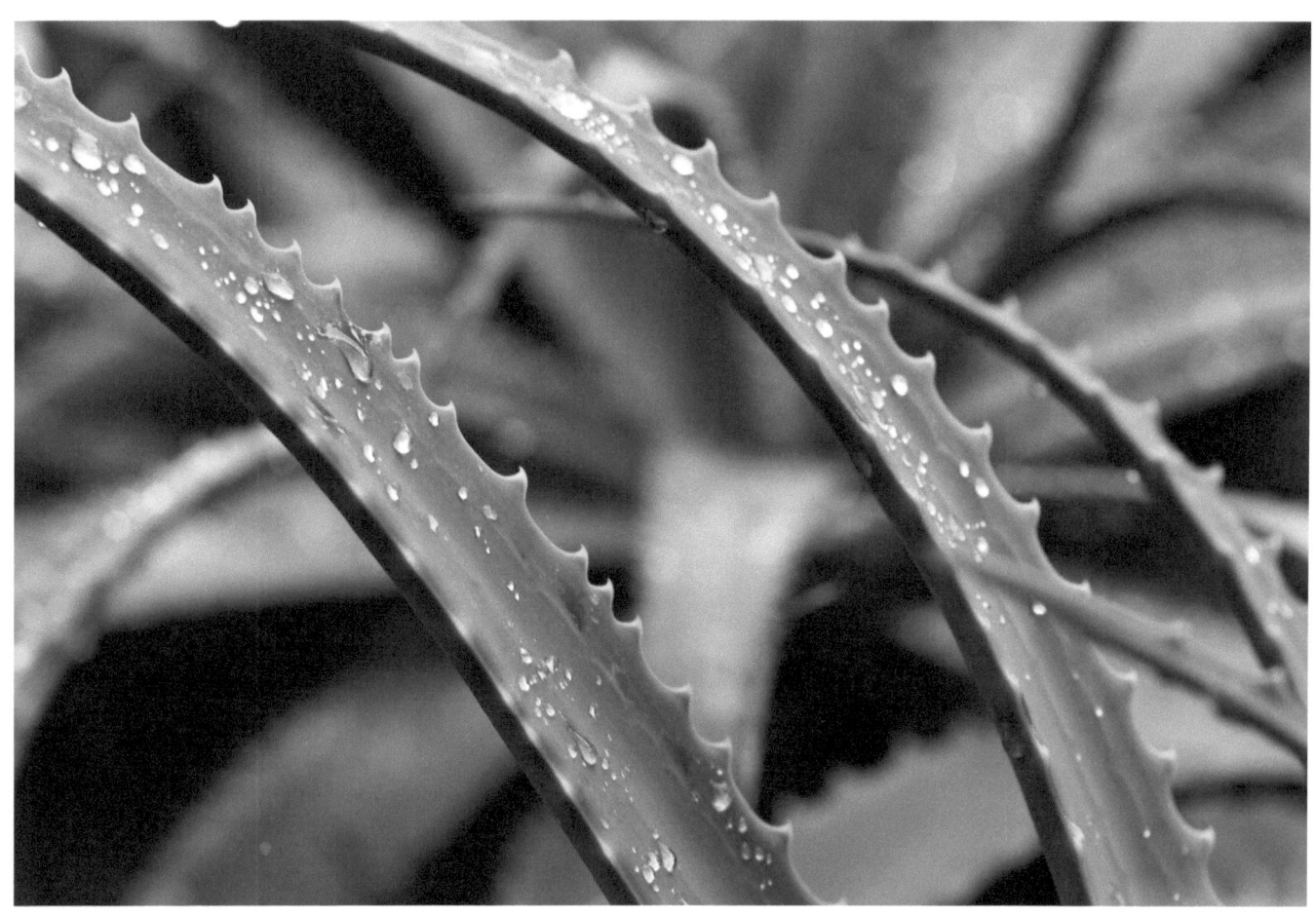

5784

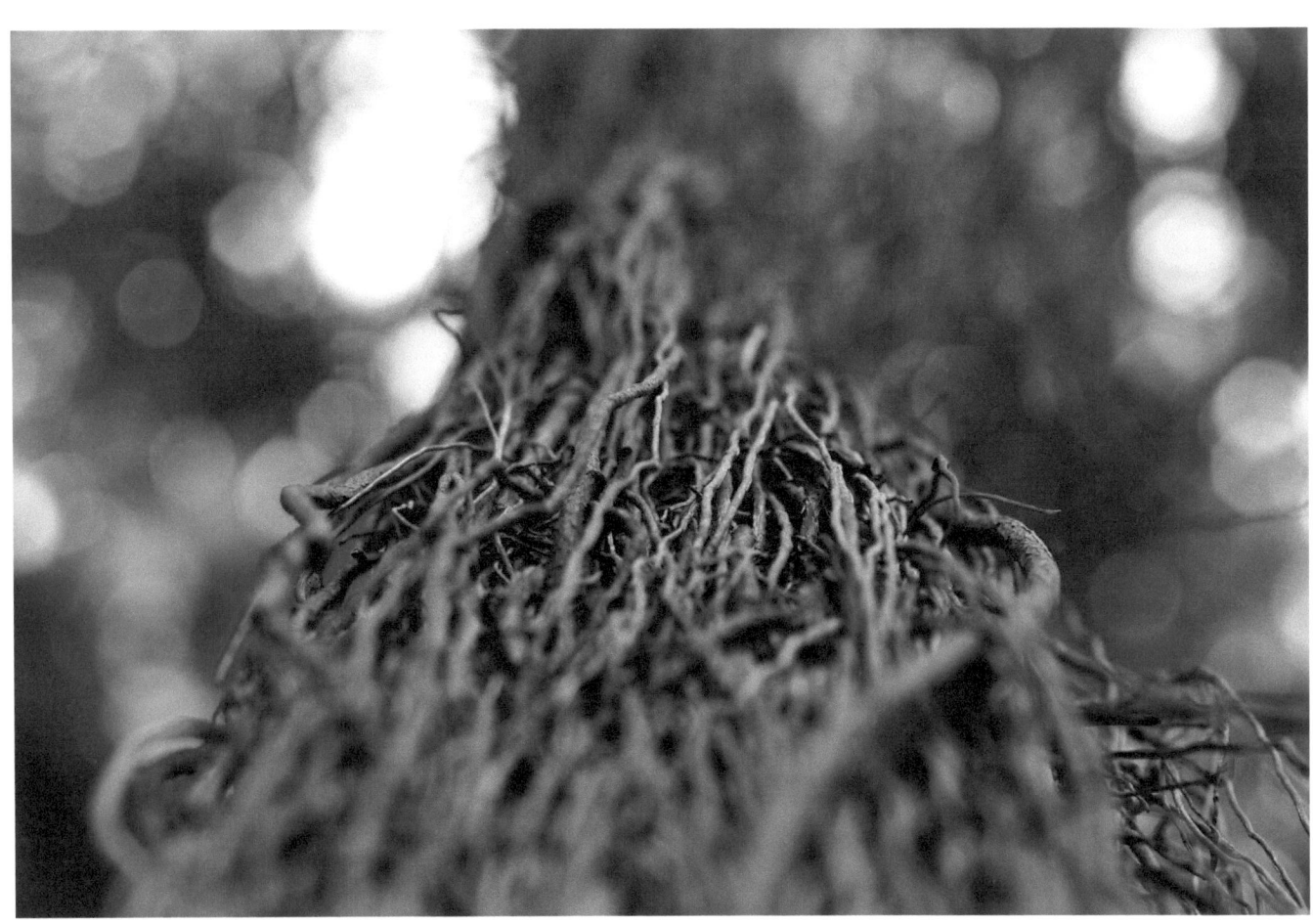

5811

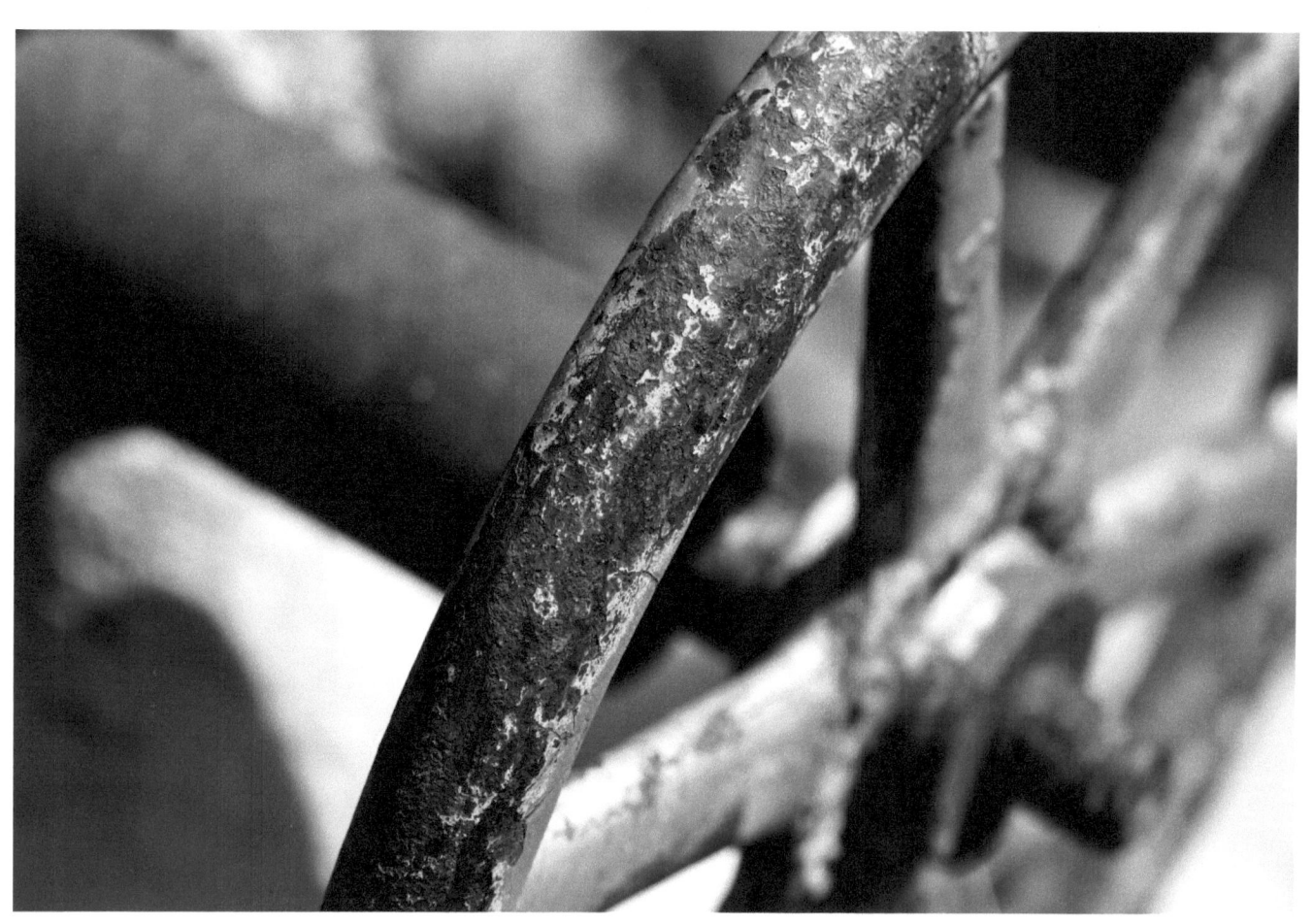

6095

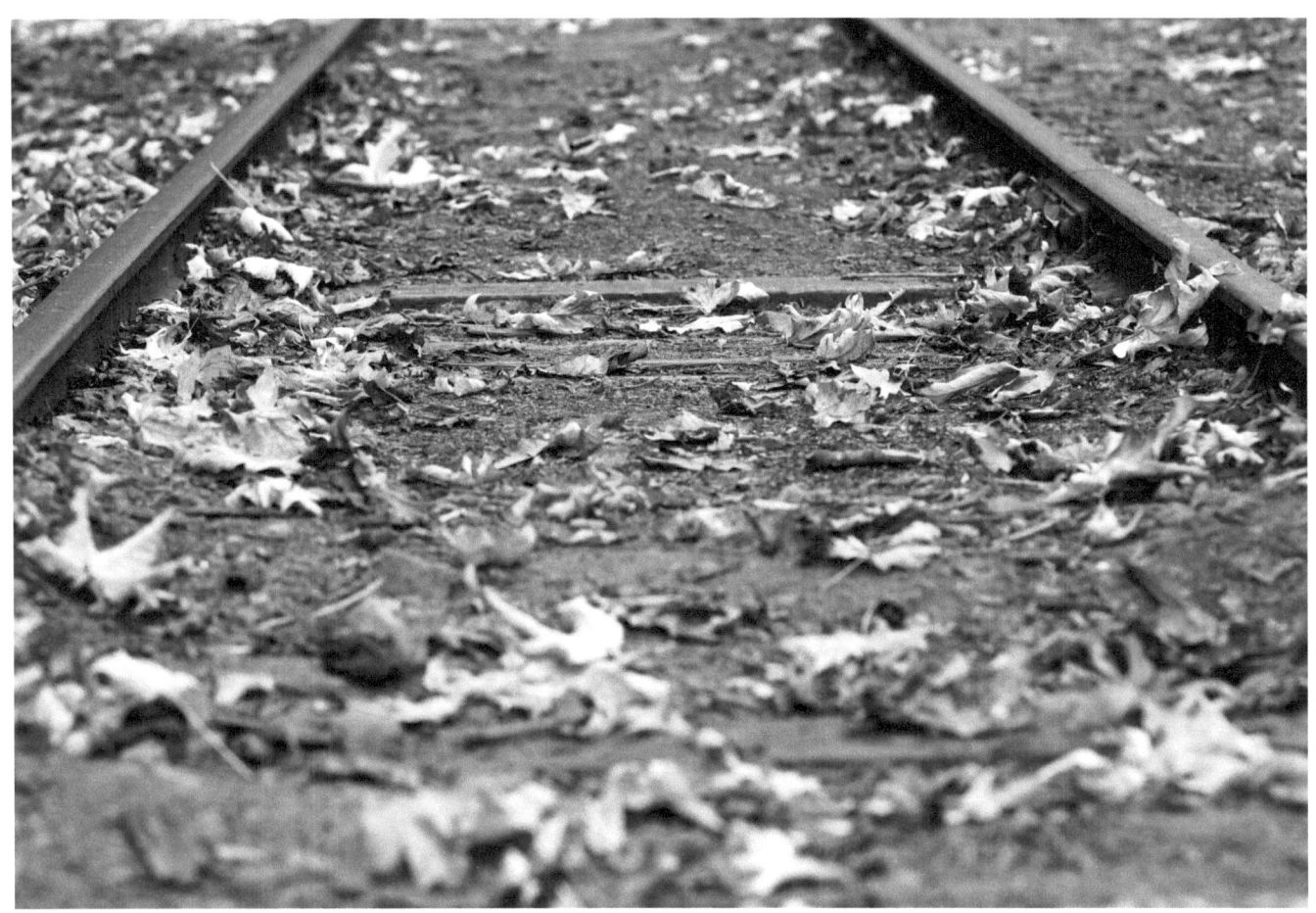

6176

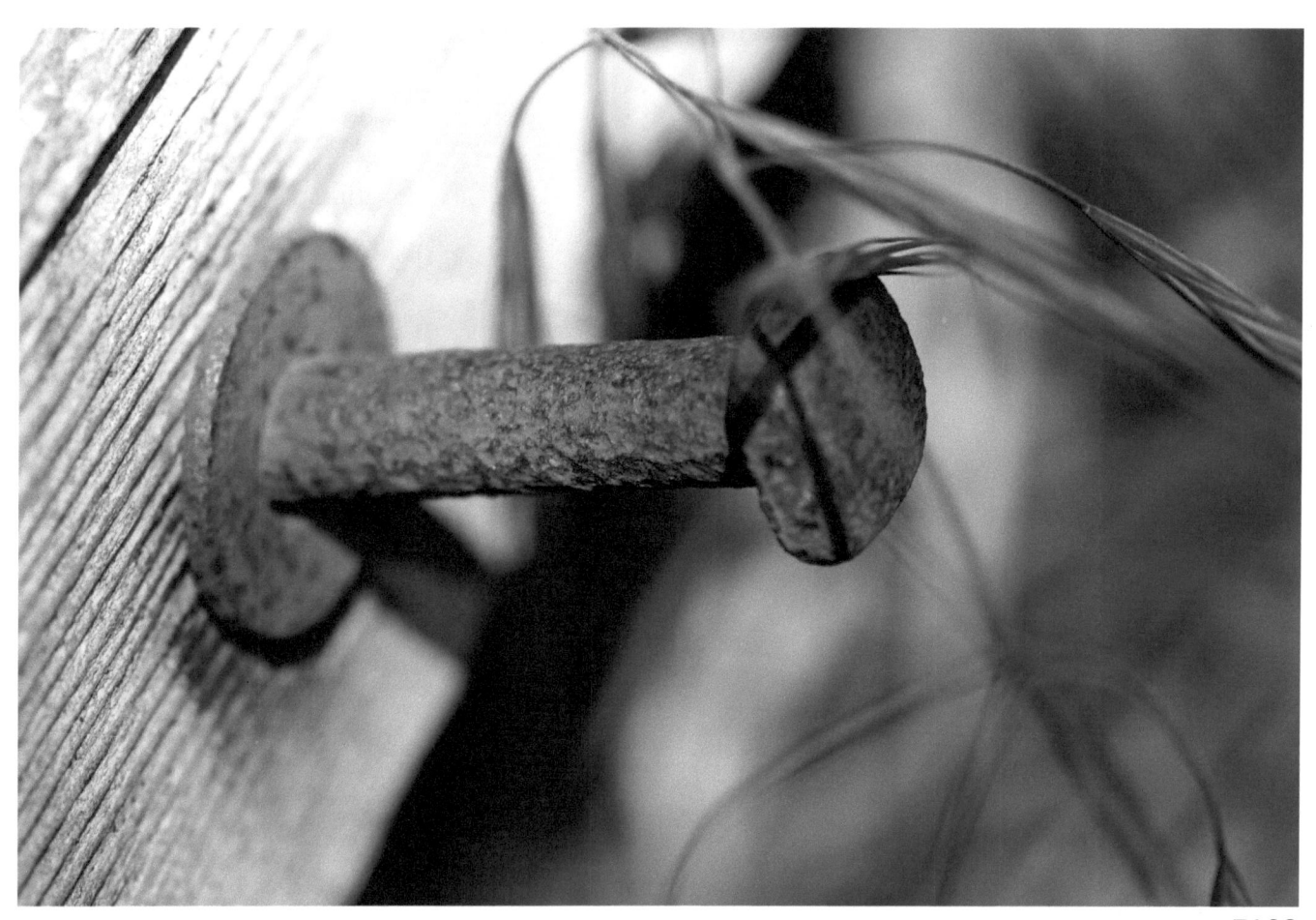

7182

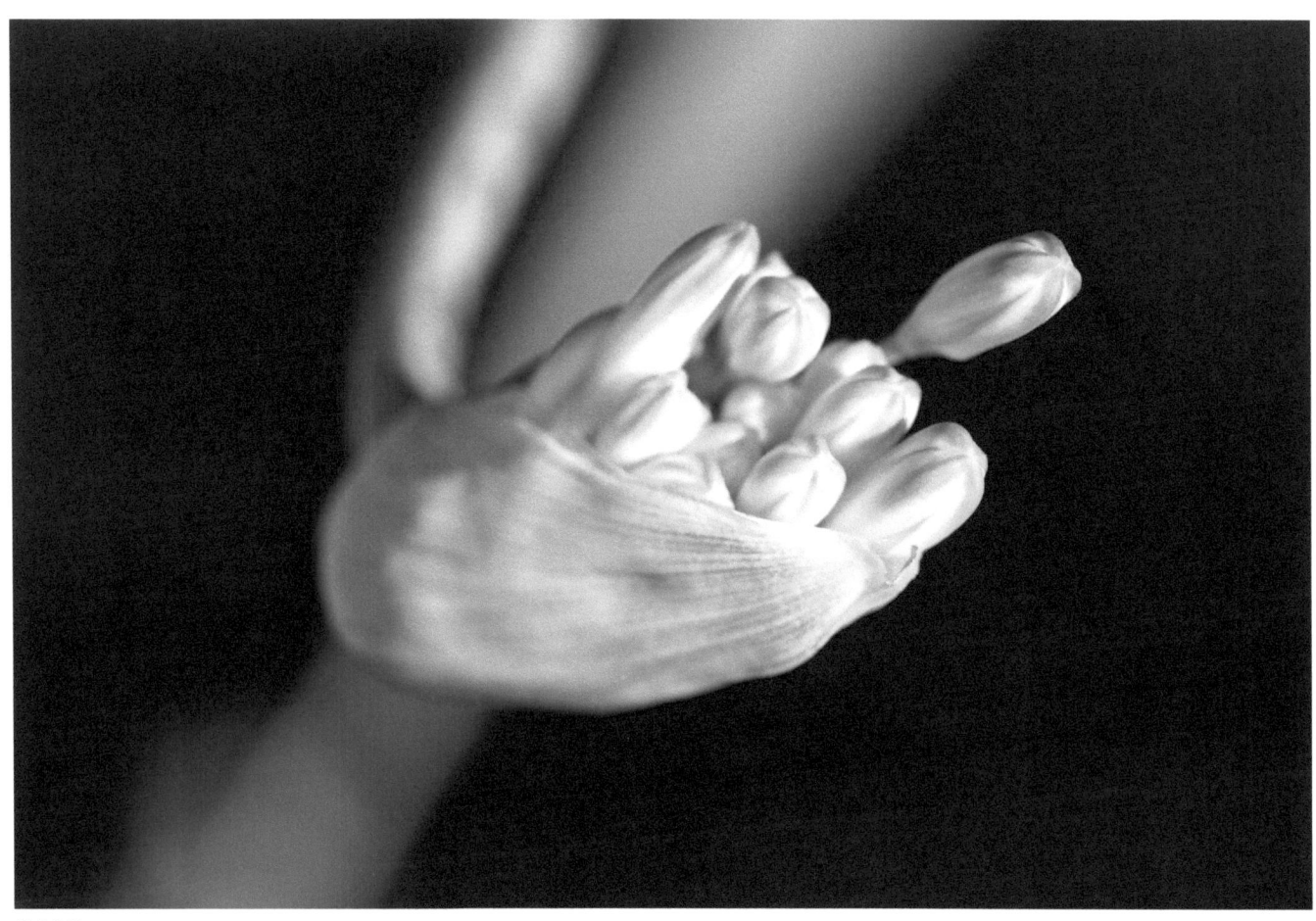

8407

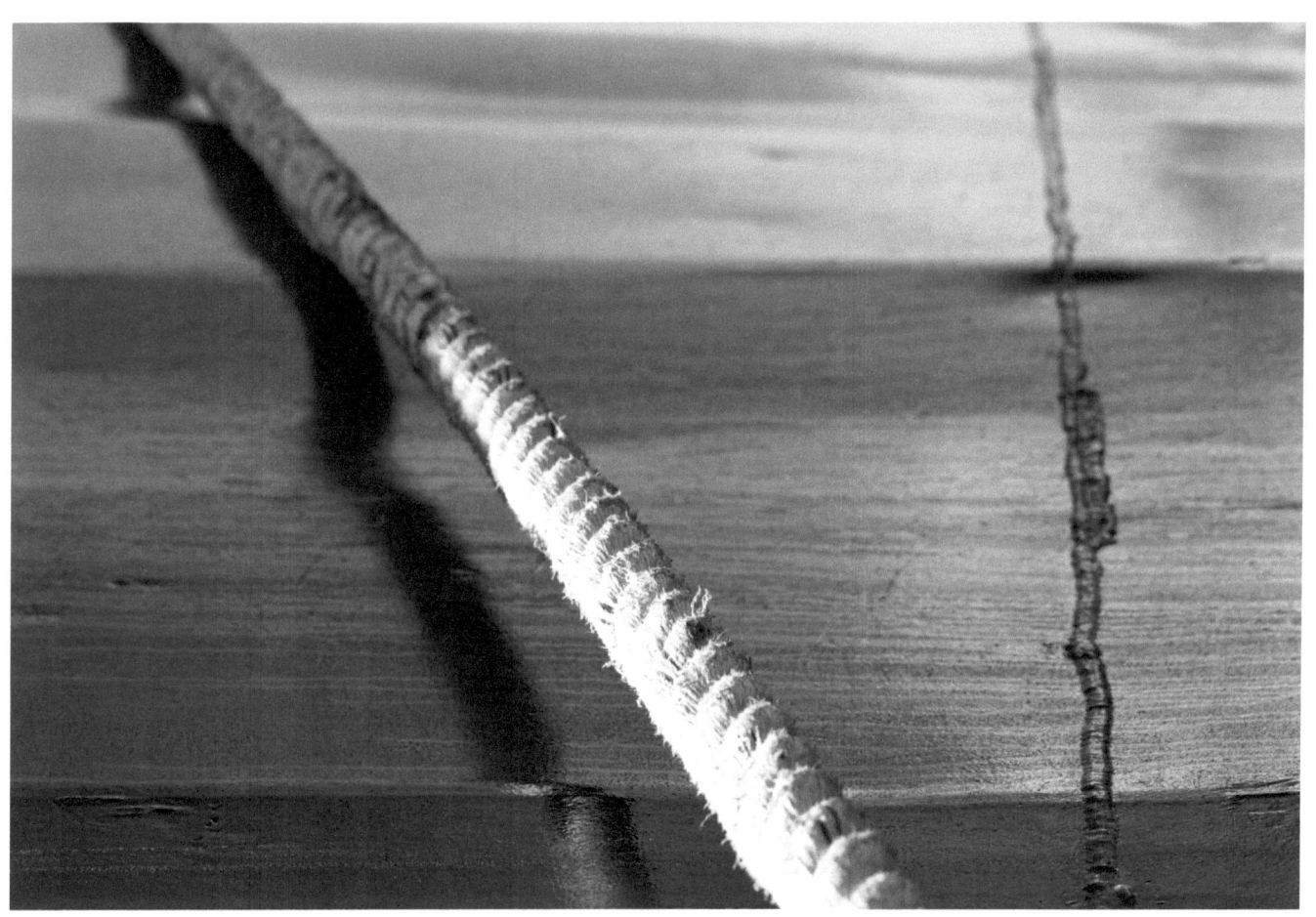

8470

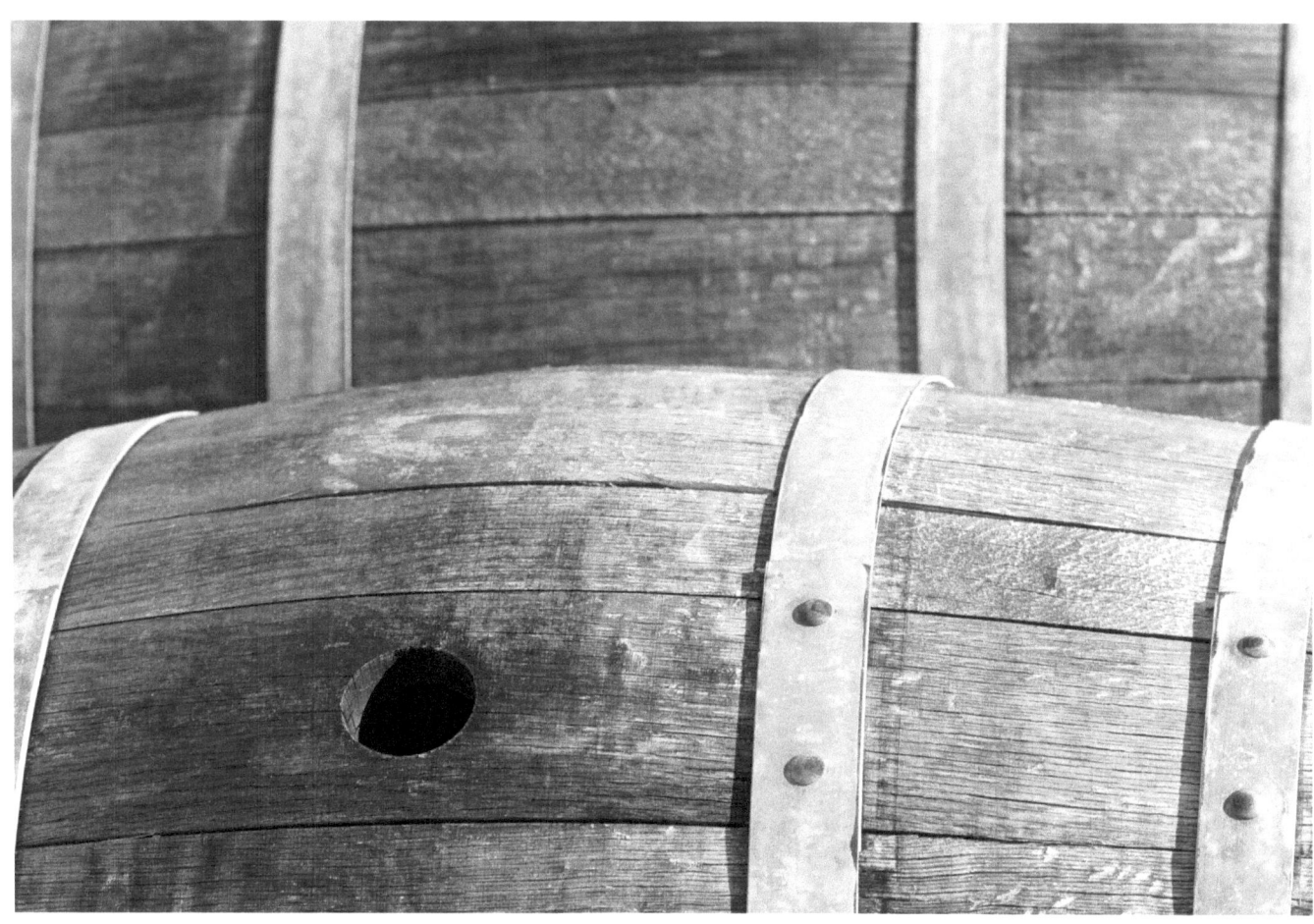

8815

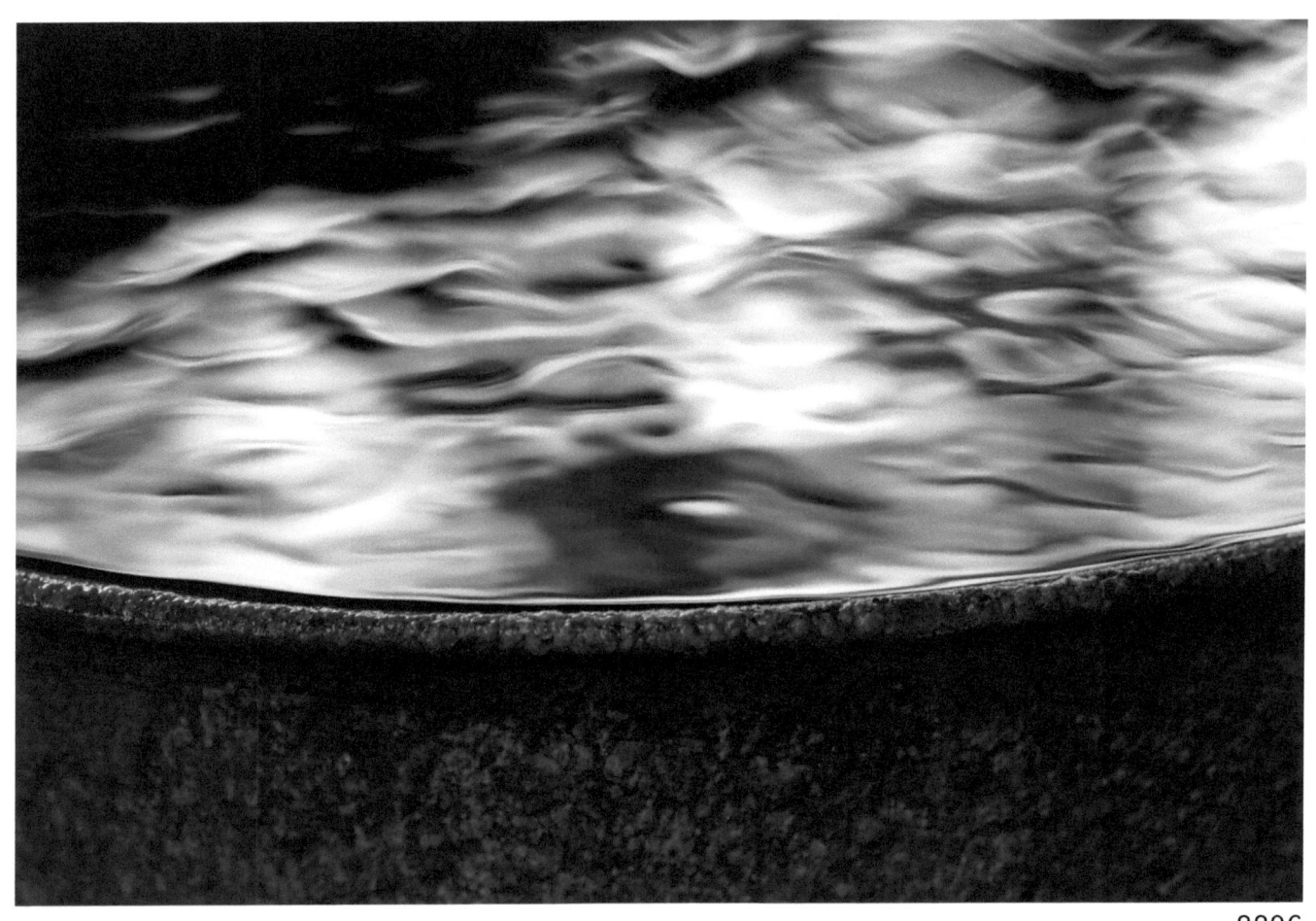

8896

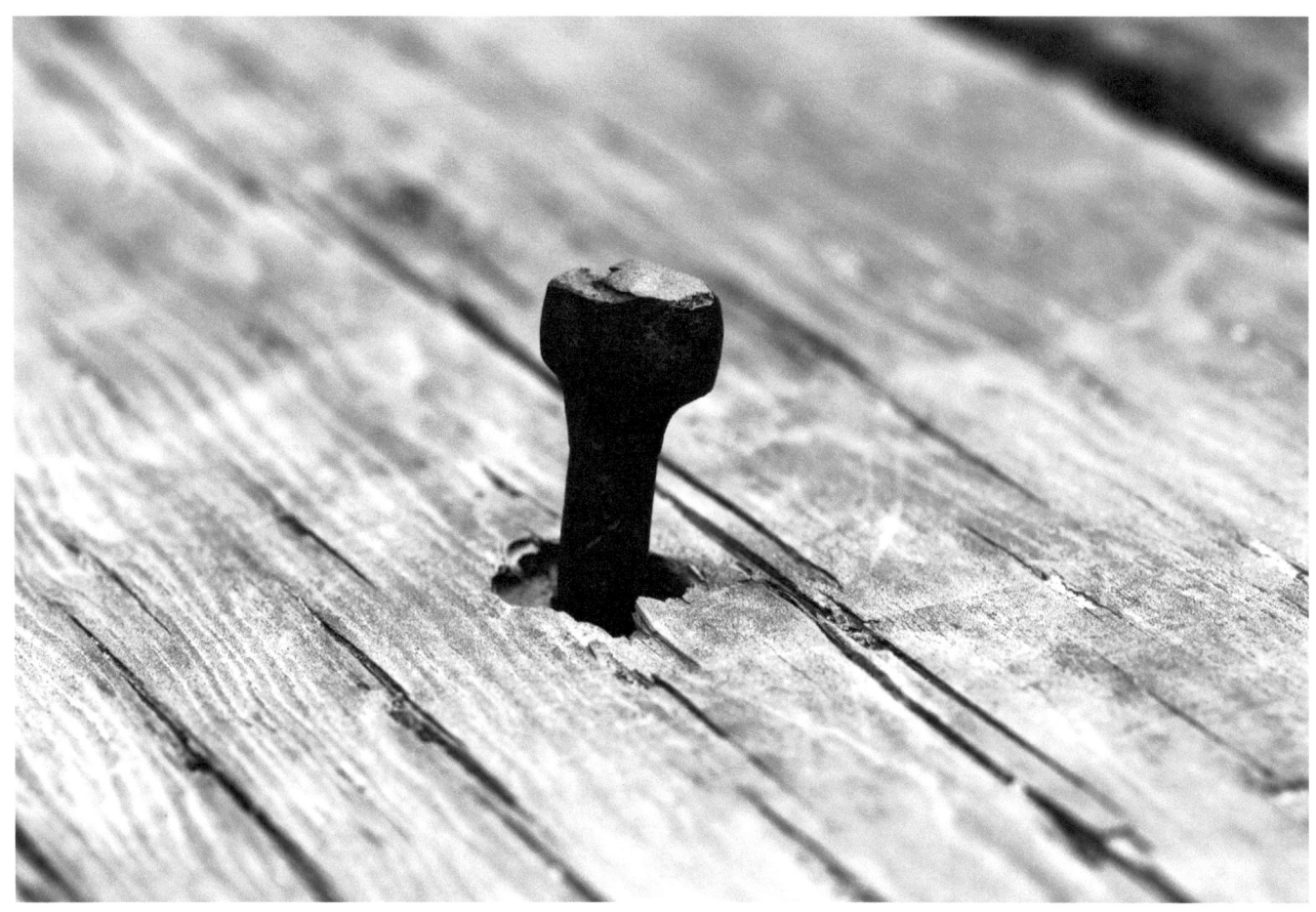

9024

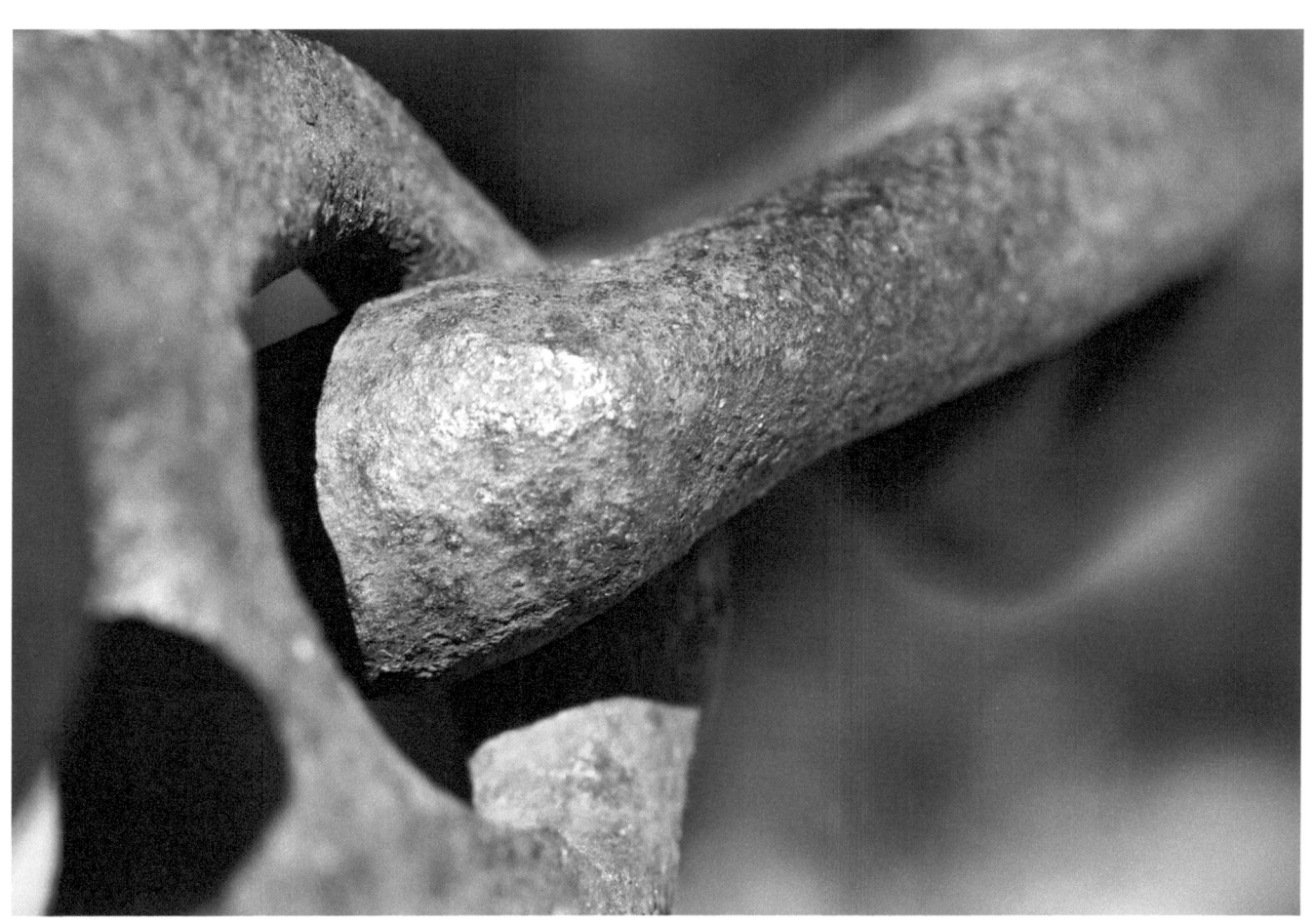

9353

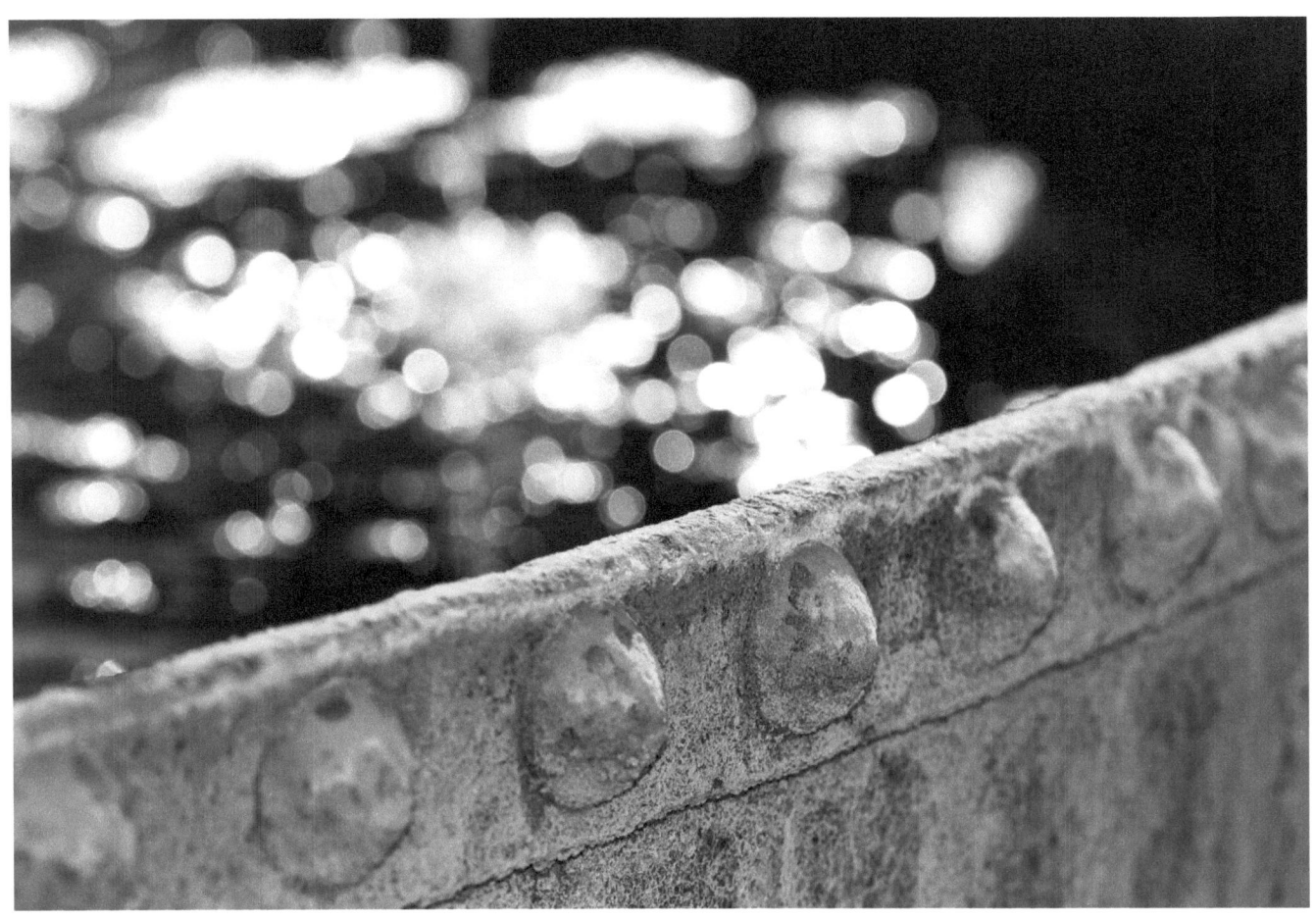

9430

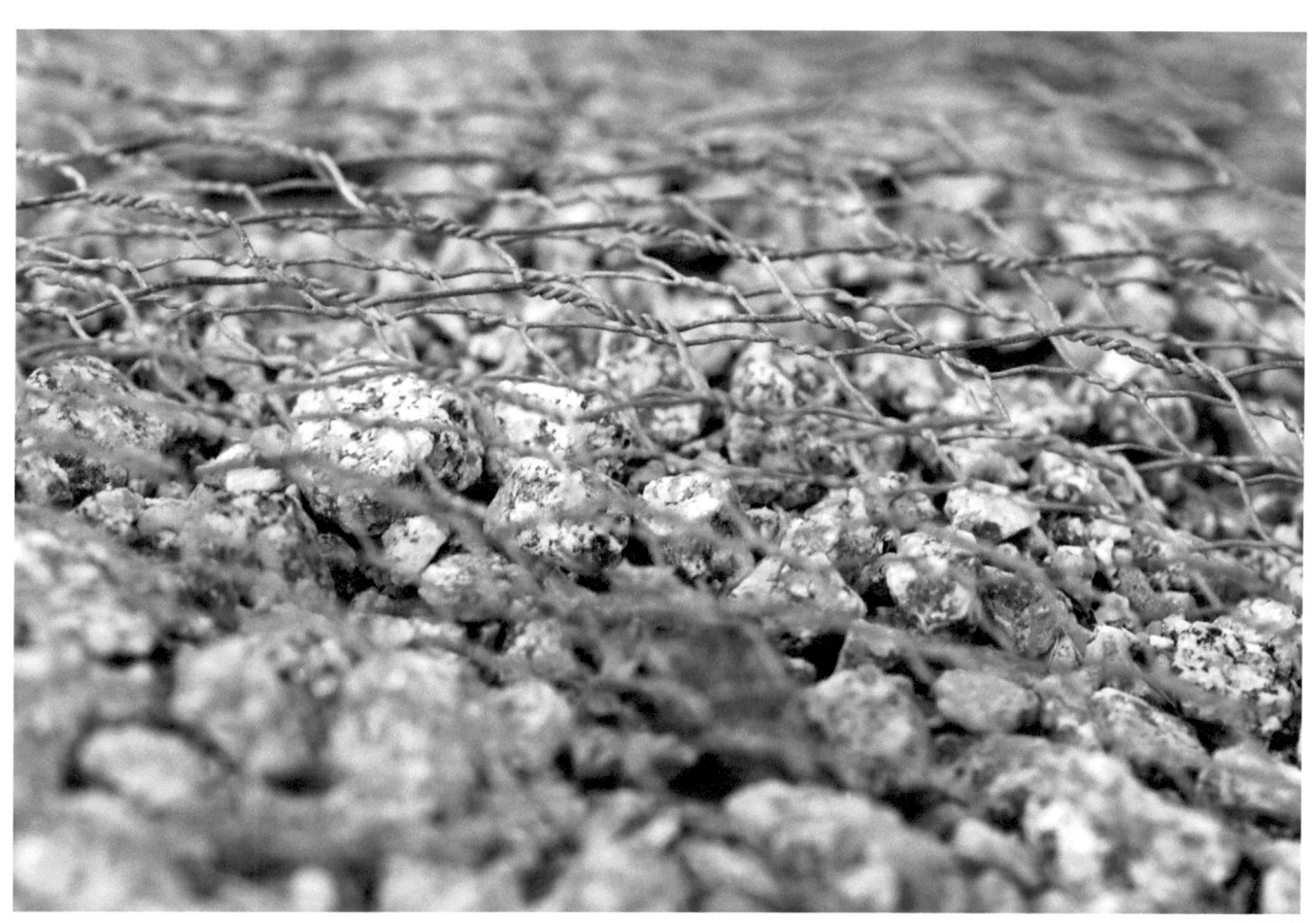

9970

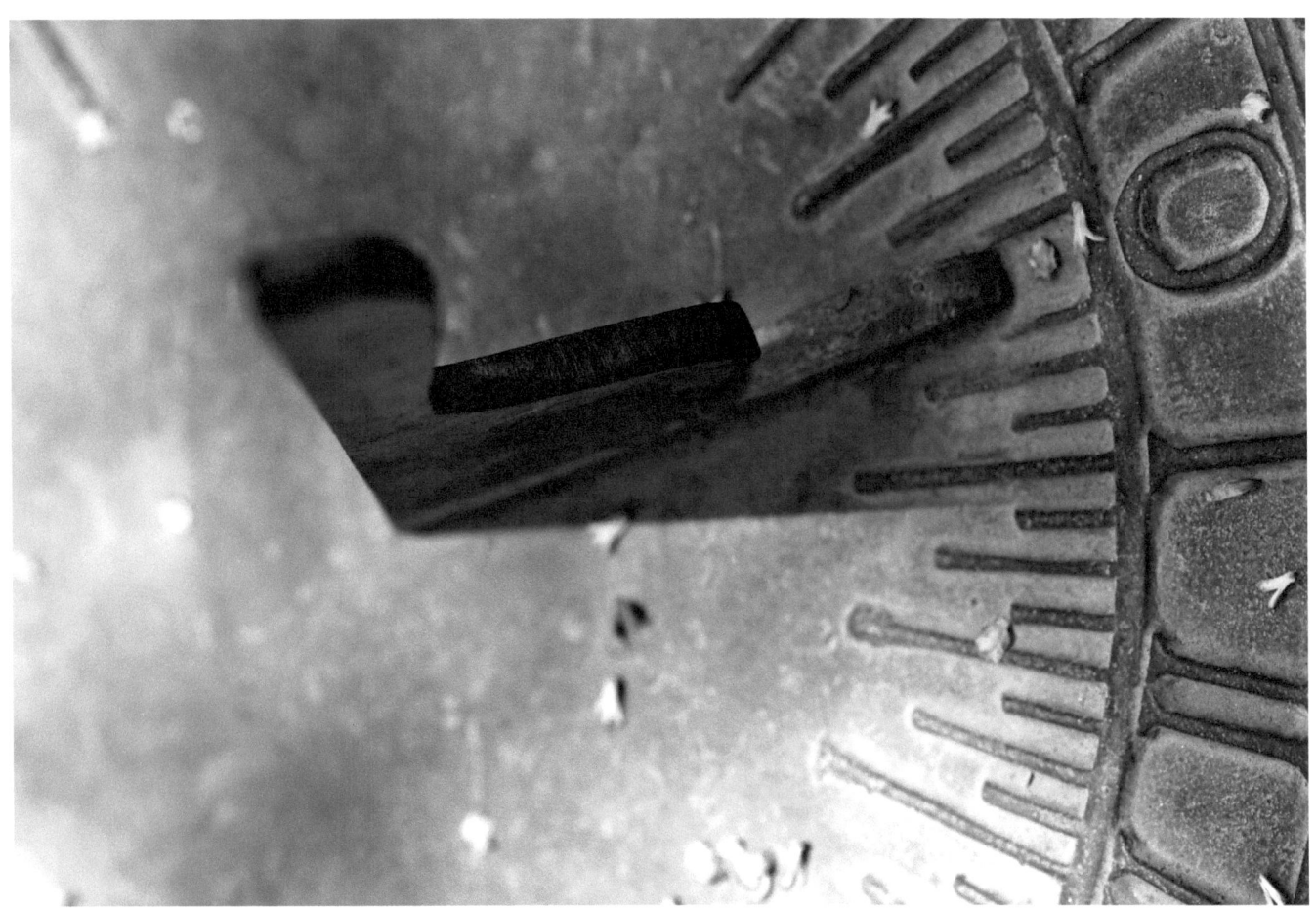

10002